Joining Lives

Joining Lives

A Primer on the Ministry of Reconciliation

Edited by
ANDY ODLE

CASCADE *Books* · Eugene, Oregon

JOINING LIVES
A Primer on the Ministry of Reconciliation

Cascade Books
An Imprint of Wipf and Stock Publishers
199 W. 8th Ave., Suite 3
Eugene, OR 97401

www.wipfandstock.com

PAPERBACK ISBN: 978-1-4982-9126-2
HARDCOVER ISBN: 978-1-4982-9128-6
EBOOK ISBN: 978-1-4982-9127-9

Cataloguing-in-Publication data:

Names: Odle, Andy.

Title: Joining lives : a primer on the ministry of reconciliation / Andy Odle.

Description: Eugene, OR: Cascade Books, 2017 | Includes bibliographical references and index.

Identifiers: ISBN 978-1-4982-9126-2 (paperback) | ISBN 978-1-4982-9128-6 (hardcover) | ISBN 978-1-4982-9127-9 (ebook)

Subjects: LCSH: 1. Social justice—religious aspects, Christianity | 2. Reconciliation—religious aspects, Christianity | 3. Religion—Christian theology, ethics

Classification: HN31. J25 2017 (paperback) | CALL NUMBER (ebook)

Manufactured in the USA   12/22/16

Contents

Contributors | vi

Introduction | ix
—*Andy Odle*

Chapter 1
Joining Lives: A Brief Practical Theology of Reconciliation | 1
—*Andy Odle*

Chapter 2
Vocation: Reconciling Our Work with the Work of Christ | 13
—*Cherie Ong*

Chapter 3
The Church and the Community | 21
—*Jim Wehner*

Chapter 4
**Backyard Eucharist: The Practice of Neighboring
and the Missional Imagination** | 33
—*Shawn Duncan*

Chapter 5
Dwelling in Union: Asset-Based Community Development | 47
—*Catherine Gilliard*

Chapter 6
**Race, Reconciliation, Recognition: A Generational Search
for the Beloved Community** | 59
—*Bruce Aaron Beard and Donell Woodson*

Chapter 7
Art and the Art of Reconciliation | 70
—*William Massey*

Chapter 8
Disability and Reconciliation: The Old Woman's Model | 78
—*Stephanie Brock and Brian Brock*

Chapter 9
Stripped Love: Reconciliation and Sex Trafficking | 89
—*Kimberly Majeski*

Chapter 10
Self-Care: A Whole New Way of Being | 99
—*Katheryn L. W. Heinz*

Contributors

Rev. Dr. Bruce Beard is the Founder/Senior Pastor of Transformation Ministries International in Jonesboro, Georgia.

Dr. Brian Brock is Reader in Moral and Practical Theology at the University of Aberdeen in Aberdeen, Scotland.

Stephanie Brock is a Nurse in Aberdeen, Scotland.

Dr. Shawn Duncan is the Co-Founder and Community Chaplain with EIRO in Tucker, Georgia.

Rev. Dr. Catherine Gilliard is Co-Senior Pastor of New Life Covenant Church in Atlanta, Georgia.

Katheryn Heinz is Co-Founder and Co-Director of CenterForm in Atlanta, Georgia.

Rev. Dr. Kimberly Majeski is Associate Professor of Biblical Studies and Christian Ministry at Anderson University in Anderson, Indiana. She is also the Founder of Stripped Love.

William Massey is the Director of Art for One and Divided Mass in Atlanta, Georgia.

Rev. Dr. Andy Odle is the Executive Director of REMERGE (formerly Church on the Street and The Center for Practical Theology) in Atlanta, Georgia.

Cherie Ong is a Business/Development Consultant in Atlanta, Georgia.

Rev. Jim Wehner is the President of Focused Community Strategies (FCS) in Atlanta, Georgia.

Donell Woodson is an Urban Community Developer and Executive Board Member of the Historic District Development Corporation in Atlanta, Georgia.

Introduction

Andy Odle

Seeds of Peace

I was sitting at a table with Stanley Hauerwas. We were in Scotland at the University of Aberdeen where I was working on a PhD under Brian Brock trying to discern the theological connections and implications of reconciliation, community, and the poor. Hauerwas was there for a meeting a long time coming. For years he had written about L'Arche and its founder Jean Vanier, but they had never met in person. This conference had been arranged specifically for this to be remedied.

For a couple of days we listened intently as Hauerwas and Vanier took turns sharing about the gentle and transformative witness of the L'Arche communities. For many reasons this conference was meaningful to me, but not least because I was wrestling with God's reconciling activity in the world and here were two influential thinkers sharing their years of hard-earned wisdom on the subject.

That conference, and the book that it produced,[1] ended up shaping my thinking more than any single source in my studies. But there was a kind of throwaway statement that Hauerwas made that also shaped my vision. At one point during the conference we divided into small groups and had conversations about what we had been hearing. I was at a table with Hauerwas when he mentioned that he had always wondered how Duke Divinity

1. Vanier and Hauerwas, *Living Gently in a Violent World*.

School would be different if there was a L'Arche community located in its center. This statement unleashed my imagination and launched me on a trajectory of thought that guided my dissertation and my living.

Nearly ten years later REMERGE (formerly Church on the Street), the organization I returned to the US to lead, continues to experiment with what it might look like if we intentionally tore down dividing walls and learned together how to be better neighbors and disciples. We continue to challenge the assumptions that ministry is best learned by the elite intending to enter vocational ministry in segregated institutions who mingle with "the people" just long enough to peer into their world for a moment only to return to their institutions to reflect with one another its meaning. We wonder what might be different if you believe you are called to serve the poor, but you actually learn from and with a prostitute, not in a special session but in due course of shared lives. We wonder what might be different if you didn't see that prostitute as a project to be learned from but as a friend, a peer, and a prophet. We wonder if you would be a better employee or a better boss if you learned from and with one another, not just skills or perspective, but life. We wonder how this joining of lives might change the way you see yourself, your neighbors, your world, and your God.

How would it change your choices, shape your imagination, and influence the communities and organizations you were a part of? Would you do your job differently if you not only believed that God was joining your life with those who had radically different stories than you, but you were actively living into that reality? What kind of dreams would you dream if you didn't accept the world as it is, deeply divided along every fault line we can exploit, but rather worked towards its reunion?

The way I understand it now, at that table in Aberdeen, Hauerwas was wondering out loud what it might look like if the institution he served boldly sought practices of reconciliation that risked the hard work of learning to give more abundant honor to those the world dishonors (1 Cor 12:23). He was wondering how such an institution might shape minds of leaders and influence the practices of the world toward joining lives.

Getting To This Point

When I returned to Atlanta I threw myself into the task of building communities of reconciliation and resistance to division. I started with three initial goals: First, move into the neighborhood I was called to serve.

Second, review what little our organization was already doing to ensure it aligned with reconciliation. Third, meet neighbors and build community with them—both individual neighbors and institutions.

As days turned into months and then years I began to grow concerned. Not concerned about my neighborhood or the violence and drugs that made up daily life. That's what led me there to begin with. My concern was directed inward toward the church. There is a long-standing critique of an increasingly disembodied faith that insists if I can just get you to say "Jesus" my job is done and I can leave you in your suffering because your problems are of your own making. We see these churches and groups every day in our Central Atlanta neighborhood and especially on weekends and around the holidays. They impose themselves on our neighborhood uninvited, assuming they are bringing Jesus with them from the suburbs or another neighborhood. They never seek to collaborate with those already at work or even as to what God is already up to; they already believe that they know what's what and who's who, and so they provide their ready-made solution to the problems efficiently during their drive-by.

It's easy if you live separate lives to make assumptions. The typical assumptions we hear over and over are that the homeless people in our neighborhood are hungry and need clothes, and they don't know Jesus. In our neighborhood nothing could be further from the truth. The amount of food and clothing that circulates through our neighborhood is astounding and so in abundance that some of our homeless friends have started cottage businesses selling the excess left behind. And if you want to know the gospel ask any of our homeless neighbors. They likely can tell it better than you because they get it presented to them over and over every day. It's not a lack of knowledge they have, it's a lack of friendship and mutually transformative love from their neighbors who visit them from afar. Imagine what could be done with the resources and time put into good-hearted but wrong-headed "ministries" if it was redirected in partnership with those who God is already using that live in the community. What if the church itself actually believed it was one?

I was once talking with a leader of a "drive-by" ministry. They come from a wealthy, predominantly white megachurch located in the far suburbs. They bring a large group of mainly white teenagers each week to provide a meal and an evangelistic worship service. One of my biggest concerns was that all the white kids served the meals to the almost 100 percent black beneficiaries and then stood off to the side to watch them eat, watch them worship, and then step in to pray with them for salvation. I told the leader that he had to at least see that the visuals were extremely troubling. He agreed. I said that if he wouldn't totally reconsider what they were doing he could at least mitigate the visual by bringing less people each week and then serve together, sit together, eat together, and worship together. Then he made an astonishing admission: he told me that he would like to do that but "the kids get so much out of doing it all." He had no real sense that he was reinforcing every division between his church and those he sought to evangelize, or at least he didn't care. Of course if all you need to do is get people to say "Jesus" then this isn't a problem at all. And the bonus is he can get the same guy "saved" every time they come down to the city.

But this sort of concern has been around for a long time. What I newly began to be concerned about was a subtle slide in emphasis from those Christians seeking to live close to the poor. Not all of them, of course, but enough that I took notice. When John Perkins began to influence the church toward a more strategically faithful expression of reconciliation he brought important and meaningful critique to the fore of the church's thinking. Many subsequent thinkers and practitioners have built on his legacy.

One of the most important correctives pressed by this movement has been in colonialist thinking and practices. Certainly not the church in the West as a whole, but a meaningful portion have repented from such activity and sought to create better ways of being Christians in the world. One of my concerns has been directed toward such a fear of colonialism that we are afraid to reveal Jesus to those who ask the reason for our work. Not a colonial Jesus, a cultural Jesus, or a bludgeoning judgmental Jesus, but the Jesus who is the origin of all things, worthy of our praise, and molding us into a new humanity. This is how I understand Paul's use of the "unknown god" in Athens (Acts 17:22–31).

My second concern is a slide toward economic development as an end in itself. Economic development is incredibly important in long-neglected communities, but when it is not born from a vision of reconciliation it becomes susceptible to the influence and aims of the world. There are certainly places of mutual cooperative activity between the world and the church, but the church must not be coopted in its eagerness to be effective. Christians must be concerned with economic development as service toward the common good, with inclusion of the most vulnerable, and in meaningful partnership with locals.

My final concern is with a sense of abandonment by some of the local church. I absolutely get the exasperation one might feel with a myriad of churches that do little more than take up space in underserved neighborhoods. The majority if not all of the membership commutes into the neighborhood for worship and vacates the neighborhood for life. I get why it might be more appealing to start your own church or stop going altogether. But I wonder if at least in some instances we can take the same attitude toward these neighborhood-located churches as we do with the neighborhood itself. Just as we are willing to patiently engage the long fight for reconciliation and justice in the neighborhood revealing in the process God's presence already there, maybe we can do the same with our commuter neighborhood churches revealing to them that God is turning their attention to reconciliation and justice in and with the neighborhood.

What I have also discovered along the way is that there are scores of Christians with some of these same concerns. Some of us in Atlanta and beyond began to have formal and informal conversations about collaboration, support, and learning from one another. Over time REMERGE decided to host a gathering for those of us who were seeking to orient our lives and work through a commitment to reconciliation. We call it The Academy for Reconciliation and Justice and it is a gathering where all are welcome, especially the most vulnerable, and a handful of thinker-practitioners share how they are working toward reconciliation through their particular ministry or vocation. We pray together, eat together, learn together, and have some fun together. This book is born from that first gathering in the summer of 2015.

In what follows you will find thoughtful engagement with each topic, not from a theoretical reflection but from hard-won insights on the front lines of life and ministry with those who are disparaged and disregarded. We all are wrestling with what reconciliation means in particular contexts. The first chapter addresses what we think we mean by reconciliation in the first place. Chapter 2 takes us on a path of vocation discovery and freedom. The role of the church in the community is addressed in chapter 3. In chapter 4 you will think through how the act of neighboring can shape your missional imagination. Chapter 5 presses us to discover God's activity and gifting in distressed neighborhoods that can be built upon before we impose our dreams upon it. Chapter 6 brings us a multigenerational engagement with racial reconciliation. How does art foster reconciliation? Chapter 7 shows us. Reading chapter 8 will provide an intimate vision into the beauty and love of our disabled neighbors. Moving from rescue to reconciliation in our battle against sex trafficking is the task of chapter 9. And the art of contemplation and self-care as the power for reconciliation sums up our voyage in chapter 10.

Thank you for taking this journey with us,

Andy Odle, Easter 2016

Bibliography

Hauerwas, Stanley, and Jean Vanier. *Living Gently in a Violent World: The Prophetic Witness of Weakness.* Downers Grove, IL: InterVarsity, 2008

— Chapter 1 —

Joining Lives
A Brief Practical Theology of Reconciliation

Andy Odle

To be a Christian in the world is to align your life with what God is up to in the world. Whether you are a pastor or a lay person, a CEO or a janitor, a husband or a wife, a governor or a citizen, this is your calling. This chapter will be spent chasing down how we might engage in this alignment. In order to discern such an audacious task I first want to ask what Scripture has to say about the subject. Although there are many texts that could be discussed, Paul points us in the right direction: "God was in Christ reconciling the world to Himself, not counting their trespasses against them, and He has committed to us the word of reconciliation" (2 Cor 5:19). God is reconciling and sending out reconcilers. In order to get at the core of reconciliation so we can be in the world aligned with God's work that we have been committed to, it will be helpful to go back to the beginning to understand the content and shape of the world that is being reconciled. I'll do this by way of John's Gospel account.

"In the beginning was the Word, and the Word was with God, and the Word was God. He was in the beginning with God. All things came into being through Him, and apart from Him nothing came into being that has come into being . . . . And the Word became flesh, and dwelt among us . . ."

(John 1:1–3, 14). John is helping us to understand the unity of reality by connecting the incarnation, the Word became flesh, with the creation narratives of Genesis where in the beginning God spoke all reality into being. The Word of God in the beginning, says John, is this same Word made flesh we know as Jesus.

Although a fantastic theological claim, how does this move us toward discerning concrete action? What is the content of God's speaking? What is he saying that is embodied in flesh and is the source of reality? Fortunately Scripture has the answer. An expert in the Law approaches Jesus and asks about the most important word God has spoken, "Which is the great commandment in the Law?" (Matt 22:36) He could have asked, like the psalmist, which is the great precept, testimony, word, judgment, statute, or ordinance? (Ps 119). Jesus answers, "You shall love the Lord your God with all your heart, and with all your soul, and with all your mind." I can imagine the lawyer thinking that Jesus has finished answering, but then Jesus says, "Hold on, I'm not finished yet." Nonetheless, he continues, "The second is like it," that is to say, the second goes with the first, they are joined together, "you shall love your neighbor as yourself." It is as if Jesus is saying that you cannot claim you love God and hate neighbor. If you were to do such a thing you would be a liar, because loving God and your neighbor is inseparable (1 John 4:20).

At this point in Jesus' response I can again imagine the lawyer beginning to walk away believing that Jesus is yet again finished. But Jesus has more to say, something quite amazing, "On these two commandments depend the whole Law and the Prophets" (Matt 22:40). For our concern this exchange seems decisive. It is not simply that these two words of God are the greatest, it is that they are not really two at all, but essentially one, and not only that, they are actually all that God has to say. All of Scripture, God's recorded speaking, depend, or "hang" as the King James Version puts it, on the Word or command to love the other; the Divine Other and the created other. All God says is "love" and Jesus is the literal embodiment of that love. The Ten Commandments tell us as much: they are commands telling us what it looks like to love God and love our neighbor.

We can now return to Genesis, as John has shown us, to understand through the incarnation the content, shape, and telos of the world that is being reconciled. When we read that God spoke all things into existence we now know that what he was speaking was "love." He wasn't creating for the sake of creating and he did not speak like some animatronic robot continually and monotonously repeating "love," rather because he is alive and interactive, he speaks love in context and with purpose. So when he says "Let there be light," it is not that he does not say those words, but rather that the entire content of those words is love.

With this content in mind, as we walk through the creation narratives we get a clearer picture of how God's word of love gives shape to the world. The first thing God speaks into existence is the space and material surroundings that will contribute to make up the environment and create place. This speaking builds over several days and as it is happening we are left in suspense as to what God is up to, but then it is revealed that all of this speaking is intended to provide the perfect environment for the habitation of his image. The environment is created to sustain the flourishing of life in general, but of humankind primarily, by fostering loving relationships with God and other creations, and also by providing for the physical sustenance necessary to survive as bodily creatures.

There are a few aspects of the environment and place that are of particular importance to highlight before we move forward. The first is that the environment does not inhibit or disrupt the flourishing of life, but actually provides for the flourishing. The second is that by speaking the environment into existence it is already filled with content; that is to say it is created to love God and in doing so proclaim his glory. For instance, when Jesus enters Jerusalem and his followers begin to worship, the Temple loyalists insist to Jesus that he must shut them down. He responds by saying that if He were to follow their wishes the stones would worship in their place (Luke 39–40). Paul tells us that if we refuse to acknowledge God we are without excuse because creation witnesses to him (Rom 1:20). He also tells us that creation groans for freedom in Christ (Rom 8:22).

After God creates the material environment he then moves on to the climax of the narrative, his image bearers, humankind. God forms humankind from the dust of the earth, breathes into Adam, and gives him life. God then places him into the environment to live and to flourish (Gen 2:7–8). I will pause again to highlight two important aspects of humankind. The first is that mankind is created, that is to say, Adam is not lord. The second is that humankind is created bodily, that is to say, humankind must receive his body, as he does his life, as gift, and it must be enjoyed and honored as such by himself and other persons.

At this point in the narrative God has built the bones of created reality and infused it with content through his Word. Now he will begin, with his creation, to give shape to the way of living as creation. Because God's command is love it is impossible to be autonomous individuals—we are created for community, joined with God and with others. As we encounter others and respond to the command to love them uniquely, over time ways of loving begin to become established. The creation narratives reveal how these ways of living are fleshed out.

I have already shown that God's speaking brings about a material environment for mankind to inhabit that supports and serves the flourishing of life both bodily and socially. God continues to speak as he interacts in specific moments with humankind. At one such moment God brings man to a particular place in the garden by the woods. There God reveals to the human his freedom, but also his limits. "From any tree of the garden you may eat freely; but from the tree of the knowledge of good and evil you shall not eat" (Gen 2:16–17). With thanksgiving and expected obedience man receives this Word. This kind of response by God's people to gather together to hear and obey God's Word we have institutionalized and taken to calling "church." But, the manner of gathering is not the command; rather it is that we join together for initiation and formation into the divine economy where persons are commanded to give loving attention to their neighbor and are made aware of God's ongoing creative activity and way in the world. Thus the Word brings us together to give us eyes to see what love looks like. Because we are created social our response to the command results in institutional form. Although the command may be heard as "gather to hear me," essentially God is saying, "This is what it looks like to love me and your neighbor in this particular context."

At another moment God commands Adam to name the animals (Gen 2:19). This task is given after God sees that Adam is lonely. But why this particular task of naming is important is that it brings order to the garden so that Adam can love God and his soon-to-be–intimate neighbor. With the vast number of animals present in the garden how could Adam possibly keep them straight during his search for a mate without giving them names? Without naming things we are left with disorder and chaos. Chaos left to itself ultimately leads to violence in an effort to impose order. Responding to God's command to maintain order is a way of loving neighbors that we have institutionalized and often call "government." Again, a particular manner of order is not the command, but rather that we maintain order where we are free to love God and our neighbors. Following the command to love God and our neighbors in this way ensures the flourishing of life.

God approaches humankind at another moment and commands them to "cultivate" and "keep" the garden (Gen 2:15). Cultivating and keeping the garden is how humankind contributes to the flourishing of life by serving one another and the common good. This is how the garden continues to produce fruit, beauty, and the things needed for sustenance. This is how the garden as part of the environment continues providing habitation that fosters communal and bodily life. In other words, this command is a particular way in which we are to love God, our neighbors, and ultimately serve the common good that we often refer to as "work."

In the garden, at another moment in time, God commands Adam and Eve to be fruitful and multiply (Gen 1:28). In other words, this is how you are going to love this particular neighbor—intimately join your lives and welcome children. Of course we often refer to this particular command as "family." But I think that we have sometimes been too narrow in our understanding of this command, often to the pain and exclusion of others. This command to love neighbors has more to do with welcoming, nurturing, and belonging to one another than it does with biology. No doubt biology may be a part of the command but it is not determinative. In fact, Jesus and Paul both relativize the biological aspect. Jesus proclaims that it is not our biology that determines family, but rather our relation to the heavenly Father (Matt 12:50). Paul follows suit by pointing out that our connection to one another as family is by faith (Gal 3:26). Jesus and Paul both claim it is unnecessary and maybe even counterproductive to be married (Matt 19:10–12; 1 Cor 7:8–9). This is why it is not unusual to call one another "brother" or "sister" in the church or to say "she's family to me" or "he's just like a brother."

Adam and Eve were commanded to be married and have babies. I do not presume to know the reasons of God, but certainly it had something to do with the fact that there was nobody else and God wanted them to populate the world. In fact, that is what God says (Gen 1:28). But Christians also certainly believe in adoption. We better believe in it as a way to be family if we are gentiles (Gal 4:5).

As we continue to hear God's command at particular times in particular contexts, our lives begin to intersect in myriad ways, not just as individuals but as communities. These ways are made of practices and institutions and values and systems and cultures and societies that are dynamic and continue to mold and morph over time. These countless personal and corporate encounters begin to give shape to the world and create place. Place is where relational connections are made and identity is formed. It is where we are welcome and belong. Place is where we are known, understood, and accepted. It is where our lives are oriented and our obligations and duties are defined. Love is not simply a one-off action, it is a way of being in the world.

But we must not leave the creation narratives too soon. Had society progressed in the garden in the way that I have described the world would look quite different. Unfortunately it did not progress in such a way because of sin. If the foundation of all reality is God's command to love the other, for our lives to be joined, then sin is being divided or separated from the other. Sin names broken relationships, the ways in which we break them and the powers that thwart the joining of lives.

As God commands us to love the other, sin tries to confuse the command or convince us there is a better way (Gen 3:1–7). There is an active war between grace and sin for our souls and for our world. So when God speaks the environment into being, sin immediately goes to work: "Does beauty really matter? Shouldn't speed and efficiency be your guiding principles?" Or "Do sidewalks really matter? Wouldn't it be easier to drive and move away to wherever you desired rather than to risk serendipitous encounters with strangers and be confined to one community where you are bound to family, place, and neighbors?" When we are enslaved to sin the powerful are free to design the environment in ways that divide us off from one another and keep us segmented and separated.

When sin enters in not only are individuals divided and set against each other, institutions and systems also become instruments of brokenness. The church is formed and sustained by God commanding us to join together for worship, discipleship, and witness; it is a place where we learn the things that make for peace while we become less and he becomes more. But when set upon by the power of sin the church becomes a place to confirm our own ways of being. It becomes less a place to hear God speak and be to be discipled in the practices of loving neighbors; instead it becomes a place to network, retreat from the world, or build our own kingdoms. Instead of freeing us to be ambassadors in the world, it demands all of our time and money leaving only disembodied techniques as witness to Christ.

When sin pounces government becomes less a way to maintain order and ensure justice, and instead becomes how we impose our will upon the weak and maintain strategic control over others. Work becomes less about how we serve one another and the common good, and more about how we get rich, even if we have to lie or take advantage of others to get there. Jobs are simply a way to make money and have little to do with vocation. Instead of family being about welcome and nurture it becomes a burden and something to be cast off; it becomes another way to control others for our own desires.

As the battle between grace and sin rages we are left unable to clearly hear God's command or see it lived in time and context, but our lives nonetheless continue to intersect in myriad ways, unleashing the lordless principalities and powers that blind, deafen, and enslave humanity, deforming the world into distorted systems and ways of being. These ways are made of practices and institutions and values and systems and cultures and societies that are dynamic and continue to mold and morph over time. Unleashing the lordless powers leads to systematic displacement and the normalizing of humanity as strangers. Sin is not simply a one-off action, it is a way of being in the world.

It is those that are cast out from flourishing in a deformed world that Scripture refers to when speaking about the poor. Poverty is not about money in your pocket, rather it names the ways in which someone is marginalized. The widow, orphan, disabled, sick, mentally ill, foreigner, and stranger are prototypical poor because they are without relational bonds in their place and thus inhibited in their flourishing. This marginalization likely leads to less money in their pockets, but the money is a symptom of a relational and spiritual reality.

Thankfully the story does not end here. There is good news! God's will is that all would be saved from sin and death; that the world and those that dwell therein would be reconciled to him and to each other (1 Tim 2:4). Throughout time this has been God's purpose. But it was not enough for God to send prophets and Law and judges. It was not enough for God to work through governments and institutions. He must come himself. Emmanuel, God with us. So at the fullness of time, in a particular place, through a particular people, the Word became flesh and dwelt among us. We call by the name Jesus (John 1).

Here he taught us not simply God's way, but that he is the way. Here he lived and died. Here he was resurrected and overcame sin and death while freeing us from their power and enslavement. Here he ascended to the Father and sent his Spirit to empower us to live and witness to the freedom he delivered. Through him we are forgiven of our sin and reconciled to God and to our neighbor; we have been given eyes to see and ears to hear that

Jesus is Lord and that we are free to love God and our neighbor. *In him our lives are joined together, not so I can be like you, but so we can be fashioned into a new people, a new humanity, a new way of being together.* By him we have been given the Word of the ministry of reconciliation.

We have taken significant steps forward in discerning concrete action toward reconciliation, but there's still some distance to go. A brief look at the story of the Good Samaritan alongside what we have covered so far will move us in the right direction (Luke 10:25–37). The Good Samaritan is broadly the story of the great reversal of the question, "Who is my neighbor?" This question is what prompted Jesus to tell the story. Much has been written and preached about this central story, so I just want to highlight a couple of insights that are important for discerning action. First, I want to draw our attention to how Jesus reverses the question. As Jesus brings his answer to a climax he in effect tells the man that he has asked the wrong question. In God's economy the question is not an external question about who your neighbor is, but rather it is a personal examination about your own status as a neighbor. In other words, not "Who is my neighbor?" but rather, "Am I a neighbor?" Asking this second question removes any posturing on the worthiness of the other to receive your love and relationship.

Second, Jesus suggests that central to being a neighbor is our active attention and suffering with those who suffer or are cast out of the flourishing of life. When Jesus asks about the characteristic of the actor in the story that gives him away as a neighbor the response points to compassion. Jesus says to go and do that. To have compassion for someone is not to feel bad for them or to pity them, it is to enter into their suffering with them. To have compassion like the Samaritan is to take on your neighbors' suffering just as Jesus takes on your suffering; to make their problems your problems.

If the life, death, and resurrection of Christ gives us eyes to see and ears to hear the Word of love, then the concrete way in which we will see and hear has something to do with our attentiveness to those who suffer. Indeed, Jesus tells us that to encounter him is to be with those who are least in the estimation and actions of the world (Matt 25:40). This is not to say that Jesus is not encountered in other places with other people, but there is something extraordinary about his presence with the outcast. My sense is that it is because Jesus' heart is broken by the suffering of his creation and so he has compassion on them. He is with them in their suffering, so if you want to be with Jesus then that is where you will find him. Many people come to visit our work in Atlanta and then go home and complain that they don't feel as close to Jesus as they did when they were our guests. I tell them that they were literally close to Jesus in the guise of the poor during their stay in Atlanta, but when they went home they went back to their old ways that keep them far away from Jesus. He's not missing, the powers have hidden him, and their lives avoid him.

All this suggests that we can discern concrete action toward reconciliation if we begin by seeing. Wherever creation is not yet reconciled, where brokenness is still experienced, the evidence will always be the suffering of those who are left out. We may not immediately see the powers that keep the systems of oppression in place. We may not see the particular actions of people and organizations that lead to suffering at any one time or over history. But we can see people and persons of lament, living in isolation and suffering the effects of being cast out from the flourishing of life. Wherever we see elements of our surrounding environment getting in the way of our connecting with neighbors or whose beauty has been stripped and no longer points us toward the Creator, then we know we have work to pursue. Wherever we see people or groups of people barred from hearing the Word with the fellowship of the church because of their dress, race, class, or the way they speak and act, we have work to pursue. Wherever the most vulnerable are hidden away and made invisible by laws, ordinances, or systems, we have work to pursue. Wherever persons are dehumanized as mere economic actors tying their worth to wages and contributions to the tax base, or are forced into exploitation, we have work to pursue. Wherever neighbors are unwelcome, abused, neglected, or treated as objects, we have work to pursue.

Not only are we being given eyes to see, we are also being given ears to hear. As a husband, if I want to love my wife well, I better learn to listen. We need to do better listening to those we love and serve; to our neighbors. Otherwise, as is often the case, we try to impose our love on our neighbors the way we want to love them rather than listen and learn how to best love them. Imposing our love on our neighbors is more about loving ourselves in spite of our neighbors. But on the other hand, we are not actually given ears to hear our neighbors. We are given ears to hear what the Lord is saying. So, for instance, if a friend comes to me after an extremely difficult personal time and just wants to die, I am not going to kill them. Instead, I am going to try and discern the voice of God speaking the word of love through them.

To be a neighbor like the Good Samaritan is to see the suffering of your neighbors and to hear the command to concretely love them. To be sure, being a neighbor is to not only be seers and hearers, but doers of the Word. But if we listen closely to Jesus tell us the story we can hear him highlighting another often unmentioned element to loving neighbors and being reconcilers. By contrasting the responses of the Priest and Levite with the Samaritan, he was not simply reversing our expectation or even highlighting individual behavior, he was calling into question an entire system that casts people out. If the priest would have helped the man would we be talking about the Good Priest? I don't think so. The priest stopping to help the man, though a good work, would not have called into question or resisted the powers and systems that enslave people in certain ways of being.

Likewise, sometimes our own good works actually maintain the status quo. For a suburban church to come down to our neighborhood, hand out a sandwich, and say "Jesus" to the homeless man, only then to retreat to their safe distance, is to maintain the status quo. The homeless man gets to eat a sandwich delivered to him by someone he has no connection to while the suburban church gets to go home feeling good about themselves and affirming to themselves what good work they are doing, while actually maintaining their false assumptions and changing nothing. In fact, they'll do it all again next week or month. The act of doing it ensures that they will do it again; it is literally self-sustaining mutual dysfunction. Or for someone to make their "living" off the suffering or exploitation of others and then blame the "system" to ease their guilt, is to maintain the status quo. Everyone is playing their respective roles in the script that allows for the world to stay the way it is currently. A good work based on the assumption that our lives are not being joined together through that act can never be an act of love. "Am I a neighbor?" is the question, not "Did I work within the system?" or "Did I do good deeds?"

Once our lives are joined together with our neighbors, especially our most vulnerable neighbors, we will not only seek ways to love one another well, we will also look for the systems and ways, the principalities and powers, which form a world that divides us in the first place. We must not only help the poor, we must ask why they are poor, and *how we personally participate in the practices and ways that produce poverty and maintain divisions.*

For lasting change to actually happen, to align our lives with God's reconciling work and not simply momentary relief, the powers must be resisted, disruptions to the status quo must take place immersed in God's alternative narrative about how he is joining lives together, along with real alternative supporting practices, systems, and communities. Our way of being in the world must be challenged and transformed because our way has created a world that casts people out. There must be a new way, a new humanity.

Reconciliation Indicators

At REMERGE we are passionate about doing what we think we are doing. So we are constantly reviewing our practices to see if they are actually fostering reconciliation or if they are getting in the way, always aware that what may be faithful today might not be tomorrow. John the Baptist had similar concerns. When John hears rumors about Jesus' work he sends his people to check into it (Luke 7:19). They ask Jesus if he is the "Expected One." Jesus instructs them to go back to John and tell him what they have seen and heard. He then provides a list of outcomes that were actually happening that he had previously detailed that people could anticipate if he was indeed the "Expected One."

Likewise, we have come up with five key reconciliation outcomes that we think can be observed if reconciliation is happening. No doubt there are others, but these are the ones we find particularly meaningful. If these outcomes are not happening then our practices and systems are not doing what we think they are doing.

The first indicator is collaboration (Rom 12:4–5). If we are one in Christ and members of one another then this should be reflected by working together toward common goals and vision with other Christians, churches, organizations, businesses, etc. The second indicator is the inclusion of the voice, contribution, and influence of the most vulnerable (1 Cor 12:22–26). We can hardly say we take seriously the ministry of reconciliation if we claim to love the dishonored of the world and then tell them to sit quietly in the corner while we who have honor make decisions for them. The third indicator is diversity (Eph 2:14). Jesus tears down the walls between groups that were previously divided and that should be reflected in our communities and organizations by the presence of people that have historically lived separated from one another. The fourth indicator is reciprocated participation of all members (1 Cor 12:4–7). Everyone has been gifted to serve one another and the common good. This should be reflected by concrete participation in the community through both giving to and receiving from one another. The final indicator is changed ways of living (Eph 6:12). This is not simply about moral actions, but rather the transformation of whole patterns of interacting in the world and with neighbors. Because we are directed to "struggle" against principalities and powers, this attentiveness should make us aware of our complicity in the systems and ways of the world, and thus result in repentance.

The shorthand is simple: our lives have been and are being indissolubly joined together in Christ, and they should look that way.

— Chapter 2 —

Vocation

Reconciling our Work with the Work of Christ

Cherie Ong

Growing up, I often thought of the work of Christ in terms of personal redemption. My experience of church revolved around this concept of "salvation," "repentance," and a process of "sanctification" that was focused on a kind of personal morality that whilst it could not be earned, revolved around being better "Christians"—reading the Bible, praying, encouraging one another to be people of integrity, and then making disciples of others in order that they would do the same. Somehow this step and repeat process was meant to transform us from the inside and help us become more "Christlike." If applied well at the collective level, these same steps were presumed to subsequently bring transformation to a community that would then grow closer together in Christlikeness. What this meant was that, at least at a surface level, a growing church was a kind of "sign" or "manifesto" of the work of Christ advancing in tandem with his kingdom objectives. There was very little dialogue about how in fact our work tied in with these objectives apart from where it involved prayer breakfasts, being upright, evangelism, and tithing the money earned from work back into the church.

Fast forward twenty years later. After graduating from college in Australia with a business degree at age twenty, I join the ranks of the corporate world at a reputable international management consulting company. My family is running a first-generation migrant church that is growing quickly and I am involved in almost every aspect from youth ministry to music and administration. I became very adept at wearing different hats but there was a growing sense of dissonance between my corporate work and what I perceived at the time as the higher more spiritual calling of ministry. Eventually after five years, the dissonance became irreconcilable enough for me to leave my job to pursue seminary in the US. However even with a master's degree in religious education and many years of full-time ministry subsequently under my belt, I could not reconcile this question of work and vocation within the framework of the church's narrow vision of redemption.

The problem is that understanding one's vocation is a lot more complex than simply doing a job to make a good living. The latter can be executed without a lot of thought or meaning behind the tasks. It does not call for a more holistic perspective of the context or obligate any scrutiny of the systems that are created or perpetuated by corporate behavior. In fact, in many cases, simply "doing your job" becomes the very justification for ignorance, apathy, or even intentional detachment in order to appease any potential grievances on our conscience. With a lot of practice and very little convincing, it is easy to see why this kind of work (albeit unsatisfying at times) can become an attractive possibility, especially if it leads to a comfortable lifestyle of convenience or wealth.

Vocation on the other hand requires discernment—not just at the individual level but also at the systemic level. It means recognizing and wrestling with evil not just within ourselves as fallen beings, but also within the systems in which we participate through our work, constantly critiquing and navigating where we are called to be agents of Christ's transformation and where we are called to relent in order to remain faithful. This is a more intricate process that requires us to understand our work and the work of Christ in much broader terms. This type of redemption stretches way beyond freedom from personal sin and slavery and leads us into a *position of freedom from an entire system that enslaves.* This is Christ's kingdom in its purest form expressed in every act and expression of work that comprises our world. Seen from this perspective, our vocation becomes a process of reconciliation whereby our work is perpetually striving towards an alignment with the work of Christ.

Freedom in Work and Living with Unveiled Faces

Paul in his Letter to the Corinthians commends us to live in this freedom that Christ has brought to us through the new covenant. When we see this in light of our striving for alignment through the process of work, the picture that emerges at the end is one of revealed glory and likeness to Christ's image.

> Therefore, since we have such a hope, we are very bold. We are not like Moses, who would put a veil over his face to prevent the Israelites from seeing the end of what was passing away. But their minds were made dull, for to this day the same veil remains when the old covenant is read. It has not been removed, because only in Christ is it taken away. Even to this day when Moses is read, a veil covers their hearts. But whenever anyone turns to the Lord, the veil is taken away. Now the Lord is the Spirit, and where the Spirit of the Lord is, there is freedom. And we all, who with unveiled faces contemplate the Lord's glory, are being transformed into his image with ever-increasing glory, which comes from the Lord, who is the Spirit (2 Cor 3:12–18).

I often come across people who say "I just need to get through the week" or "I'm trapped in a dead-end job." The result of sin has made our work seem worthless, mundane, and dull, and in even more extreme cases, we see entire industries built around systems of greed that are evil and oppressive. For the Israelites, these systems are reminiscent of their life in Egypt and "the veil" is what prevents them "from seeing the end of what was passing away." It is the unveiling that leads to freedom through the Spirit of the Lord. This is what gives us hope. It is such a hope that enables us to be bold—bold enough to contemplate the Lord's glory with unveiled faces so we continue to be transformed into his image.

It is important to note that this process of transformation is something that comes from the Lord and this is the very work of Christ, reconciling us with his image, the Imago Dei. What this means is that it is not our work that brings about the transformation but our *obedience*. Our responsibility is to *turn to the Lord* and live with unveiled faces. There we will find freedom in work, and hope and boldness to reflect his ever-increasing glory.

As alluded to in my introduction, this process of "turning to the Lord" has often been seen as some kind of religious repentance that happens at church through a lot of confession, reading the Bible, and attendance at services. While these are all aspects of our spiritual life, we need to understand that the process of repentance necessitates our whole being of which a large part of that is our vocation. This is a difficult thing to do especially as we live in an industrialized age where everything can be neatly separated into different compartments. We like to think that our spiritual life does not need to mess with our work life. We don't like to mix business with church or vice versa. Furthermore, the church as an institution seems to have also embraced this cultural change as if to protect itself from the pitfalls of society and segment its role to that of things that relate only to the more "sacred" matters.

Traditionally, this was not the case. When God called his people out of Egypt, they were called to a new kind of life together still functioning within a system of work. When we look at the example of the early church, there is no sense of separation of personal life—"this is what I do on the weekends"—and their vocational lives. Even as recently as a couple of centuries ago, there was no such thing as the corporation, only systems of government and churches that were an integral part of the overall economic system.

We turn to the Lord when we recognize that there is a sacred process of transformation that takes place in every act of obedience. That includes the way we are obedient both individually and corporately, and not just on a Sunday or in our family life but also within our system of work. The image of Christ includes one where work originally was not intended to be laborious but operated in a life of freedom as a means to demonstrate Christ's glory. Living with unveiled faces and contemplating the Lord's glory is us looking at our existing contexts and understanding where and how Christ is calling us with our specific skills and gifts to operate boldly as agents of Christ's transformation for the benefit of his glory. It is discerning where God is already at work in the world transforming people and systems to more closely reflect himself, then having the confidence to act in concert with his work.

This is of course, all easier said than done. The reality is that our existing contexts are fraught with complexity, cultural expectations, and family constraints; the world around us is difficult to parse and there is a lot of grey when it comes to vocational choices. In some industries it is hard to see any higher purpose and particular jobs can become so detached, specialized, or transactional that any original purpose behind the system of work has either been lost or thwarted. Take for example the insurance industry. If you look at how it evolved, it was originally meant to assist people in times of unexpected need. Communities decided that if each person set aside a little bit of money, then if one of their neighbor's homes burned down, they would all have enough money to assist that neighbor to get back on their feet. Much of the insurance industry that has evolved as we know it today is a system driven by the maximization of profits at the expense of true social good. Insurance companies evade claims, protect themselves with fine print and exclusions, and the worst of them use fear tactics to sell you their products. We need to ask the question: what is the original purpose, the underlying Imago Dei, the meaning that brings reconciliation between our work with the work of Christ?

Doing Good Works, or Reconciliation through Work

At this point it might help to pause and discuss briefly the difference between an emphasis on good works and the process of reconciliation through work. For many Christians in the workplace and Christians who run businesses, there is an underlying assumption that regardless of what their business or role in the business is, as long as they are abstaining from unethical practices and setting aside some money to individually or corporately perform good works, every thing in between is not of significant importance. Basically what this means is that individuals and companies can maintain their primary goal of continuously maximizing profits because by inference more money means potentially more good works. To clarify, I am defining this category of good works broadly to include things like donating to the church, charitable organizations and different causes, volunteering for a ministry/service project, or helping friends and family members in need. These are all worthy investments of money, time, and energy but what they sometimes detract from is the primary goal of bringing about reconciliation through *the essence of the work itself*, whether that relates individually to the workers themselves or corporately to the organization as a whole.

If God's primary concern was to generate resources to enable good works to carry out his actual mission, then arguably the goal of every Christian (or Christian business) should be to find the fastest way to get rich. And even then, there would be an endless justification to become increasingly rich without any real gauge of how much would ever be enough. I have affectionately named this syndrome after Bill Gates since I have now met so many Christians who point to Bill Gates as the epitome of "good in the world" and use him as a justification for all sorts of questionable or inattentive practices. This "Bill Gates Syndrome" reinforces our need to generate as much money as possible in order to do as much good as possible to make the world a better place. It may not be wrong to be rich or even just earn a lot of money by virtue of your vocation, but there is something fundamentally flawed when the money-making and the doing good are separated. Such a case becomes a self-perpetuating cycle: one act demands the other. The problem is that this kind of dualism does not necessitate a genuine assessment of (a) how money is made through the fundamental system of work or (b) one's underlying motivations. Instead, the end of "doing good" (as worthy as whatever that cause may seem) somehow justifies the means.

What if neither making money nor doing good work is the primary goal? An emphasis on the reconciliation process through our work demands that we look deeper at our practices and motivations. It requires a more thoughtful and daily commitment to faithfulness that centers on choosing to act in concert with the work of Christ that is both transforming us and our system of work in order to bring us as individuals and a collective people closer to the Imago Dei. It is not dependent on either our effectiveness or capability to make money or even perform good works. This is a more difficult path of discerning our life of engagement with the world, compelling us to identify and face our frailties and the frailties of the systems that surround us whatever our context. You could be a housewife, a farmer, a banker, an engineer, or a pastor—brokenness exists in different forms and looks very different in each of these scenarios. Sometimes it expresses itself in the form of the abuse of power, the sway of greed or fame, the undermining of human dignity, or the ease of passivity. Our work is that constant striving towards reconciliation or the reversal of brokenness within our context, so that Christ's glory becomes a natural manifestation. This is subsequently where we find ourselves most fulfilled at work.

Finding Your Own Journey of Reconciliation

When I left the corporate world to pursue ministry, I thought that my calling was to serve the church directly through ordination or indirectly by physically ministering to those living on the margins. After completing my masters in religious education at Trinity Evangelical Divinity School in Chicago, I returned to Australia determined to stand in solidarity with "the lower ranks of society." I joined the unemployment line at welfare services just to feel what it was like to go through a system of dependence. I removed everything from my resume to apply for hospitality jobs serving coffee and waitressing. Then I volunteered the rest of my time to the local church and other not-for-profits that led me to a high-poverty neighborhood fraught with issues of generational unemployment and consisting of a large mix of asylum seekers from Somalia. These were special times filled with moments of joy and pain as I became friends with some of the most unlikely characters—an unemployed senior lady who was an alcoholic but proved to be the most amazing chef I have ever met, a man with mental illness who could never complete a task that well but was always willing to serve, and an Anglican priest who had the most outlandish idea to sell his century-old church in order to build a community hub in the middle of the run-down strip mall where the unemployed and the refugees intersected.

To make a long story short, after a few years spent persevering in this neighborhood, I relented. Even though I was successful in helping the priest secure over half a million dollars in grant money from the State, this money was never disbursed because there was so much disparity about the way it was to be spent. Sometime towards the end, I found myself in a heated disagreement with the Region's bishop, and saw face-to-face the dysfunction of a century-old system, which subsequently led me to discontinue my ordination. I left this phase of my life with a lot of disappointment, questions, anger, and pain. On one hand this was a failed project, but on the other hand, I was encountering a whole new freedom I would have never experienced at a high-level "desk job." It was this freedom that allowed me to not only empathize with those living on the margins, but allowed me to recognize both failure in myself and in a system that represented the church.

Around the same time, I met some Christian businessmen who later became significant mentors and colleagues. They were instrumental in moving me forward in my spiritual journey in a context that I least expected—in the workplace. I started to understand that the work of Christ calls us not to run away from dissonance but to engage with it faithfully as these are the broken systems that we find everywhere, which just like ourselves, Christ is in the business of reconciling. We began to explore how Christ's work in the world, reconciling us to himself, implied that our work is a purposeful means to that end through whatever gifts and contexts that we operate in, whether that was as a mother (which I now am to two gorgeous boys), a development worker, or as a management consultant.

Today, many years later, I am assisting a multimillion-dollar foreign real estate investment fund deploy and asset manage large commercial properties in downtown Atlanta. There have been many ups and downs and question marks, but nowadays my perspective is different. I have a much stronger sense of purpose that, as difficult as it is (and as many times I veer away from it), keeps me coming back to what matters most in light of Christ's work of reconciliation in my current context. Here in the competitive real estate industry where profits, numbers, deals, and transactions rule, I search for those who are like-minded in purpose and can see beyond the dollars and cents into the heart of a city and the life of a neighborhood, with residents and businesses that are looking for place to call their community. On this journey, I have found that contrary to what I used to expect, many of the people who are participating in Christ's transformative work do not profess Christ at all but are compelled nonetheless—a testament to the fact it is truly the work of Christ. Many Christians, on the other hand, who are devout supporters of the institutional church, are unwilling to struggle with the difficulties of reconciling traditionally lucrative real estate deals with the perceived charitable work of community development. They would prefer to keep their profitable businesses separated from their charity and their spirituality separate from their professional lives.

I can certainly say that I do not have all of this figured out. However, I have experienced a shift in my understanding of the purpose of work as it relates to Christ's work in the world. And even though I have floundered in between the maze of ministry, social justice, and the corporate world, the one thing I have found and can be certain of is Christ's freedom in working out my vocation. With this freedom, I look to Christ with an unveiled face, contemplating his glory that each day is bringing transformation to my life and the lives of others around me.

— Chapter 3 —

The Church and the Community

Jim Wehner

For a number of years now I have been intrigued by the role of the
church in community. For the most evangelical churches, the word
community has evolved into a description of fellowship. I could say, "My
church has great community," meaning that I feel a sense of belonging and
fellowship with my friends at church. Or I could even say, "This is how we
do community," which turns it into a descriptor about the way we interact
when members of the church are together. I see this as a sign of a general
slide of the church away from any understanding of a theology of place.
A theology that recognizes the importance of the geographical boundaries and the people within those boundaries that form the neighborhoods
around the church building. A theology that recognizes God is not limited
by the walls of the church building and works in the neighborhood just
as he works inside the church building with its members. A theology that
acknowledges the responsibility of the church to be a winsome participant
in the neighborhood and to bring reconciliation to neighbors that may not
grace the inside of the church building. We are often so focused on attract-
ing people into our building that we have very little idea of how to enter the
community as an ambassador and servant in order to bring reconciliation
to the streets.

As the leader of a Christian community development organization I am often asked for my thoughts on the role of the church as it relates to community development. I am not sure I have the best answers to this question, but I can say that I believe that if the church were to make some adjustments to its posture in a neighborhood, we would see an increased growth in the reconciliation of neighborhood residents. There are many reasons for why I believe that this is true. Let me start with my story to give you some background for my thinking.

The church that I planted and pastored for nine years was about two miles from a strip of weekly-stay motels. This is not unique in itself except that as God took me on a journey of ministry that included people living in these motels, my understanding of the role of church in the greater community was drastically changed. We were not the closest church to these motels and certainly not the biggest. We were a group of about seventy adults plus children. But we made a decision in our fifth year of meeting together that changed how we did ministry in the neighborhood. We decided that if we requested our members to support the work of the church with a tithe, then the church could practice the same generosity in the neighborhoods surrounding our location. We committed to giving away a percentage of our budget to various missional works. A portion of this monthly commitment was set aside to help people in the neighborhood that were not connected to the church in any way. We believed our generosity might reflect the thankfulness we felt toward God for his continual faithfulness and generosity to us.

Unsurprisingly, the weekly-stay motel is one of the places that poverty hides in the suburbs. Much of what we call affordable housing in the urban context has found its way to the first- and second-ring suburbs in this new form of affordable housing, where a hotel room substitutes for an efficiency apartment and a week-to-week rent agreement replaces a twelve-month lease. Most of us know that if we were looking for a place to stay, this type of hotel is not where we would look. The truth is that poverty is not so much hidden from the church as it is ignored.

As I began to interact with the individuals in these hotels, my sense of calling began to change and as I describe it now, I became ruined for the church. Not the church of Scripture. The *ekklesia*. I am completely passionate about that church. But the church as an organization that is unprepared to care for the poor or that sees the gospel almost solely as a transactional message has lost my interest. It simply doesn't match up with what I see in

Scripture. Within these motels I found a support community that develops among the residents, much like you would expect in a more stable neighborhood. It is not the clean and neat concept of community that we use to describe our fellowship within the church. Existence in these housing projects is hammered out in low-paying jobs and often relies on subsidies, whether government-supplied programs or church-based benevolence. But it is not a God-free existence. I found him there ahead of me. I just couldn't see beyond the chaos of the raw existence at first. I grew up in a middle-class suburban context. My family has known lean times, but we would not be described as poor. I grew up in modest homes and driving used cars. I didn't know that the very fact that I had a car—even a used car—said something about me to the groups of people that live in these motels. None of us see clearly the privilege we have until we are either in relationship with others that can help us see it, or we lose our privilege and begin to understand what we had. Can you imagine a church that handled its privilege like Christ handled his with the incarnation? "In your relationships with one another, have the same mindset as Christ Jesus: Who, being in very nature God, did not consider equality with God something to be used to his own advantage; rather, he made himself nothing by taking the very nature of a servant . . ." (Phil 2:5–7, NIV).

This change that I felt in my calling began when the church would receive calls for benevolence. As a small church without administrative staff, I answered the calls that came in each day. After a while I began to track the calls. More than 80 percent were calls for financial assistance. Individuals would literally take the phone book and cold call churches looking for help. It turned out that the majority of those calls came from residents of the weekly-stay hotels.

At first, these calls were treated with care. We prayed regularly for the people that were calling. I tried to build relationships. I wanted to find a way to connect the people in need with the congregation. Frankly, I just was not very good at it. Remember my upbringing. I am pretty squarely in the middle class socioeconomically speaking. I simply did not understand what real help looked like for these neighbors. As a pastor, I was seminary trained; however seminary did little to prepare me for ministry to the poor. Please do not misunderstand me! I am thankful for the opportunity to have gone to seminary. I loved my time of learning and study. But in this context, it did not take long for me to learn the difference between leadership in the church and participation in the community. My seminary training prepared me to lead a congregation. However, I received no training in working with the poor. No instruction as to how to decipher healthy benevolence models. In fact, I began to realize that I had never even taken the poor into account when I was building the leadership team to help me plant this church. As a church-planting team, we looked at all sorts of demographics and data, but we never once looked at where the poor were situated in our community. It never crossed our minds that we ought to be as intentional about serving the poor as we are about our youth group or small group ministry. Our goal was to plant a great church that would draw the unchurched from the entire community. I planned our Sunday services to hit with clear impact, but never took into account the fact that I left massive groups of individuals out of my planning that the Scriptures clearly show as important to God. I did this not so much by intention, but more because I did not understand what it means to live without certain resources. I was simply blind when it came to poverty. Unfortunately blindness also meant I was ignorant of the needs of many members of our neighborhood. Like many of us, I saw poverty as a weakness. It was a sign of God's hand of discipline. As I ventured into serving the poor, I found nothing was further from the truth. The rich and poor alike make poor life choices and experience the consequences of those choices. The rich and poor alike have need for reconciliation.

This is what I mean when I say that I am ruined for the church. Start bringing these issues to the forefront of the church and you will recognize very quickly that most of us love the *idea* of serving the poor. But when it comes to choosing a church location, changing the neighborhood where we live, adjusting the programs of the church such as the youth group or the children's ministry, people vote with their feet. The challenge of serving the poor is simply too demanding and painful when you are in the position of privilege. So after nine years of leading the church, I held up the white flag of surrender. Not only was I unprepared to meet the needs of the poor, I was unable to lead my church to a healthy understanding of mission that included the poor. The honest truth is that it took three years after leaving the church for me to be able to articulate my own leadership failure.

There are other, less pointed reasons that the church avoids this responsibility. The sheer amount of need is overwhelming. I was amazed how quickly word spread among the residents of these hotels that our church gave assistance for rent or power bills. Meeting one need immediately led to phone calls from others that had needs as well. As a small church, we simply could not afford to say "yes" to every caller. This tension has a real price to it. I found myself tossing and turning over decisions that I made earlier that day. I was haunted by the memories of conversations with people that I could not help.

There is also the reality of dependence. Bob Lupton, in his book *Toxic Charity,* comments on how one-way giving creates dependence, "Yet those on the receiving end of this outpouring of generosity quietly admit that it may be hurting more than helping. How? Dependency. Destroying personal initiative. When we do for those in need what they have the capacity to do for themselves, we disempower them."[1] When the church, over and over, has to fight a wave of dependency that is created by its programs, the answer is often to shy away from the program, rather than doing the hard work of creating healthy models of benevolence. I spent almost four hours one afternoon saying "no" to a woman that our church had helped multiple times. We had unwittingly become a major source of her support and she depended on us to come through when things got tight. After I had denied her request over the phone, she showed up at our church offices in a panic. She declared over and over that if we did not pay her rent that afternoon she would be kicked out. When I said no, she called person after person using the church's phone and a phone book. She cried. She yelled. At one point she stormed out of the office only to return a few minutes later. In the end she was able to pay her rent without our assistance. But she never came back to the church or asked for any further help from me. This is what it looks like when dependency is broken. It does not matter if it is dependency on drugs, alcohol, or relationship. Breaking dependency is painful and ugly. This is why churches shy away from helping.

That brings me to the heart of the matter. The church ought to be the best source of reconciliation in the neighborhood. We ought to live it like we mean it! We ought to pursue reconciliation as though there were nothing more important to us. We should understand clearly that for Christ, reconciliation meant moving into a new location and giving up the privilege of heaven, suffering and dying an agonizing death. In that light, I have tried to outline a couple of ways a church might begin to step out into the neighborhood in tangible ways and become more effective in the communities that it serves.

1. Lupton, *Toxic Charity*, 3.

The Church as Resident

I cannot say strongly enough that proximity changes how we answer questions. Solutions that seem wise and simple from the outside show themselves as arrogant and thoughtless once you are on the inside. They are full of assumptions that simply do not fit once you are working from within the community. It is time for the church to move into under-resourced communities and begin to practice the ministry of presence. The community that FCS serves is full of churches that have abandoned the neighborhood. Their buildings remain and sometimes small congregations still meet, but they are made of people that commute into the community for church. After church on Sunday, they are gone until the next week. I attend a church that left one of the wealthy parts of our metro area to work within a community of need. The relocation put us right in the middle of a neighborhood that is full of immigrants. Our church shrunk from 350 members to around seventy-five. My friend and pastor jokes about his church growth strategy, taking a church from 400 down to under one hundred in less than twenty-four months. For those of us that have stayed through the transition, we would not go back to what we had. We miss our friends that now worship elsewhere, but we also know that not everyone is ready for this type of ministry. I hope in the future that we see more and more churches making the difficult choice to move toward our neighborhoods of need.

The Church as Listener

The church would be a better neighbor if we would learn to listen as well as we preach. The unfortunate problem of seeing poverty as a sign of spiritual need is that we misunderstand some of the most faithful saints around us. When I started work with FCS in 2008, one of my responsibilities was the operation of a sixty-four–unit apartment building designed to serve low-income individuals and families. One of my favorite residents at GlenCastle apartments was an elderly woman named Rose. She was just over five feet tall and weighed all of eighty pounds. She cussed more than any person I have ever known. She was an angry person and offended many of our other residents. Life had not been nice to her and she had the toughness to stick it out. I prayed for her often, though I rarely had the opportunity to talk with her about spiritual matters. I came to work one day to find her sitting on the ground outside our corporate offices, which were in the building adjacent to the apartments. I offered to help her up, thinking maybe she had fallen. I quickly realized that she had not fallen. She sat down intentionally to protest and was not returning to her apartment until we repaired the things she wanted fixed. There was no reasoning with her. Only listening. Finally I was able to convince her to walk over to her apartment where she could show me the needed repairs. I listened for almost an hour before she was calm enough for me to leave and for the apartment manager to take over. I went on with my day. When I arrived at work the next day, there was a message from Miss Rose on my answering machine thanking me for listening to her and telling me that she loved me. There were a number of other occasions that I sat with her in her apartment just to listen. Miss Rose passed away a little over a year ago. I cannot say that she was any closer to the Lord at the time of her passing. God did not grant me the blessing of knowing her eternal destiny. But he did grant me the blessing of knowing Miss Rose and enabling me to learn from her. My relationship with Miss Rose has shaped my understanding of the cross and my own need for a savior. It is unfortunate for the church when we approach the poor as a project, failing to listen and learn from them. The Scriptures tell us that God has granted the poor to be rich in faith. I find this to be true as I listen and learn from them. Wayne Gordon says, ". . . listening to the community enables us to build relationships and to uncover the qualities, talents, and abilities the community has to address and eventually solve its problems. Listening helps community members to see themselves, not as some government program or outside group, as the source of answers."[2]

Unfortunately, listening requires the resource that has become most valuable in our current economy: time. Listening takes time and presence. Without them the gospel reach must be shortened to a tract that I memorize and repeat in a couple of minutes if I can find a way to slide it into conversation. This stunted form of the gospel avoids true discipleship that allows us to rub life against life and learn from one another. I am not saying that there is no proclamational message in the gospel story. There is. But Christ told the disciples that they would be known by their love for one another. He did not say they would be known by the number of people that made decisions for Christ. In fact, it is in the act of loving that we experience the reality of Peter's exhortation, "Always be prepared to give an answer to everyone that asks you to give the reason for the hope that you have. But do this with gentleness and respect" (1 Pet 3:15, NIV). You and I ought to hear people

2. Gordon, *Making Neighborhoods Whole*, 106.

asking us about this hope because they see the reconciled life we live! You get my point . . . the church that listens to its neighborhood will soon find multiple ways to minister to the needs of its neighbors.

The Church as Servant

It strikes me as funny that the disciples were quite competitive with one another. The Scriptures show them often jostling for position before Jesus, their rabbi. On one occasion Jesus tells them specifically that "whoever wants to become great among you must be your servant . . . for even the Son of Man did not come to be served, but to serve, and to give his life as a ransom for many" (Mark 10:44–45). The struggle for the church is that we have translated this idea of being a servant into the idea of doing service. Our service projects are planned without ever talking to the people being served. The church comes with volunteer resources, a gospel message, and assumptions about how to meet the needs of the community or individual. Recently I was speaking with a church whose neighborhood has transitioned to an immigrant population. They have been faithfully praying about how to serve the neighborhood that is now majority Spanish speaking. They have noticed that there are a high number of homes where children are left with grandmothers for daycare. They were also noticing that these homes are often rundown and dirty in appearance. As they prayed they had the vision of building a community center on their property and forming a daycare for these children that would provide clean and safe facilities. They would have curriculum that would bring the gospel to these children and they could set up ways to interact with the parents in the hope of bringing the gospel to them as well. We would all agree this is a big vision and a very generous use of their land and resources. A community center will take hundreds of thousands of dollars to build, staff, and manage. To do so on behalf of their neighbors is clearly generous. I asked them how the neighborhood responded to the idea. They had not yet found a way to have this conversation. Who would they ask? I encouraged them to address this missing piece of their process before moving forward. They picked up on my hesitancy and asked what concerns I had about their plan. After all, they were faithfully praying and listening to God. I told them that I thought the residents of the community might have a different value system. They might value family over the church's view of "safe and clean." And I told them I would bet cash money that they would react negatively to their *abuelos* (grandparents) being put out of work by the church daycare. This in turn could hamper their opportunity to bring a gospel influence into the neighborhood.

My point isn't that they should throw away this vision. My point is that they should see themselves as servants of their neighbors rather than seeing themselves as fixing their neighbors' problems. If they dedicated themselves to listening and learning they would quickly learn the key change in the relationship is happening within them, not within their neighbors. They would find a new source of love and compassion for their neighbors. We see this all the time at FCS. God's plan for us is to be more like Christ. Taking on the mission of reaching a community for Christ is to take on the mission of being formed into Christ's likeness. That means change often happens in us before we see change in our neighbors.

I was consulting with another church in a different city but with the same circumstances. Their neighborhood had transitioned over the years and the predominately white congregation was left to figure out how to participate in their surrounding community. They had a great idea. They had a connection to their city's professional basketball team. They leveraged this connection to build a state-of-the-art basketball court on their property that could be used by the neighborhood children. It was really spectacular and a huge win for the church in terms of public relations and being viewed as change agents for their neighborhood by city leaders. On the day I was consulting with them we went over to the basketball court and watched twenty Hispanic youth playing soccer on the muddy fields beside the pristine basketball court. With regular use, they had worn the grass away from the area. They had split their field into two soccer games by using their sweatshirts on the ground. The church members lamented the painful and expensive lesson of putting the service project ahead of the relational work of getting to know their neighbors. Not only was their investment sitting dormant, they were no further along in bringing reconciliation to the neighborhood.

The Church as Economic Driver

There will be some readers of this chapter whose churches have moved beyond the ministries of presence, listening, and service and are ready to begin working at starting businesses, providing jobs, and improving housing. Others may ask how these business-oriented projects fit within the work of the church. If we are trying to reconcile the fabric of an under-resourced neighborhood, then the church ought to lead the way in reconnecting that neighborhood to the greater community. This cannot be done through service programs alone. The neighborhood will need economic drivers to do this. The church has one of the best resources available to the community in terms of economic development: its people. Within the walls of the church, those who are most gifted and skilled in this area of ministry tend to be found in the congregation on Sunday morning rather than in the pulpit. So churches often miss opportunities for productive life-changing ministry because they need their congregation involved in their small group program or manning their vacation Bible school program. When questions of economic development come to the church, they immediately run everything through their pastoral leadership, which is focused on spiritual development, not neighborhood development. But take a group of real estate professionals and ask them to develop a healthy housing ministry and just sit back and watch them come alive! They will pray passionately and apply the Scriptures to the process before any leaders have the opportunity to say, "please open your Bibles to . . . ."

The church also misses an opportunity to release the gifting of its congregation because when it reads that spiritual gifts are for the building up of the body it hears this as the institutional church. Sunday after Sunday we reinforce the message that the skills and leadership exercised all week long by our members who work in the world have little to offer beyond worship and tithes. But release them into the neighborhood to redevelop dilapidated housing or to start businesses that offer strategic employment and there is an immediate multiplication of ministry at the church. Reconciliation, when done well, will impact all areas of our lives, not just our salvation. And the gifting of the Spirit is not simply meant to work inside the walls of the church.

At FCS we have worked with a real estate agent for the past eight years. She has helped us acquire and sell more than thirty-five homes. That means she has helped us bring thirty-five new neighbors into previously vacant homes in our neighborhood. She is helping to literally restore the physical fabric of our community. It has been a privilege to watch her walk out her faith in her profession. She has made us better and smarter as a housing organization. She has pushed us to build a better product. At the same time we have had the opportunity to disciple her along the way. We have been blessed to watch her grow spiritually and to see her giftedness in light of the kingdom. She is not going to lead a Bible study at the church. She is not going to start a small group in her home. But she increases the reach of our organization and the ministry of reconciliation every time she exercises her skill set on behalf of our organization.

Two years ago one of our key staff members and resident of the neighborhood decided to transform a building that we owned into a small grocery store that would bring affordable and healthy foods to the neighborhood. He talked to neighbor after neighbor and asked them about the idea. He had them list the types of foods they might want in the store. He was also mature enough to know that he is a nonprofit leader and not a professional grocer. So his next step was to gather a group of seven business and grocery professionals. He asked them to develop a plan and budget for the grocery store. He also asked them to share their professional opinion as to whether we could make this work financially. As grocery professionals, they understood the details of ordering product, merchandising a store for increased sales, hiring and training a staff, and managing inventory to reduce loss. These are all critical business components to this ministry, which now provides twelve jobs in the neighborhood as well as fresh produce and groceries. When the church views everything from a heavenly mindset, without understanding the language of business and economics, they set themselves up for financial failure that in turn hurts the people the church was serving and, in the end, shortens the reach of its ministry of reconciliation.

Salvation not only saves our souls, it makes us better humans. The ministry of reconciliation that Christ gives to us is not simply for the building of an organization; it is for the reaching of humankind. The message of reconciliation ought to enable us to live more fully and freely into who we were when Christ met us. To James and John, two of his closest disciples, Jesus said, "Follow me, and I will make you fishers of men" (Matt 4:19). What might he have said if they were IT professionals or entrepreneurs? The analogy of fishing for people worked because they were professional fishermen. It released them to see their previous work as relevant to their calling. What if our pastors and spiritual leaders understood how to do this for their church members? A church that has graduated from the skills of listening and serving into the phase of economic development in the neighborhood will extend the reach of its ministries. Reconciliation reaches beyond the individuals in the neighborhood and impacts the built environment. Healthy homeowners and businesses will naturally engage the city leaders on behalf of the neighborhood. The church that is empowering its neighbors through economic development is reaching into the structural systems of injustice in a way that most churches never even touch. Everyone benefits and reconciliation begins to look more and more heavenly!

Don't be fooled. Economic development is a slow, tedious process that requires painstaking planning and financial accountability. Economic development requires significant investment, but if you want your under-resourced neighbors to experience the benefits of God's work here on earth and grow beyond the confines of poverty, this type of development is necessary.

I stated above that when you start bringing issues like poverty alleviation and neighborhood development to the forefront of the church, you will recognize very quickly that most of us love the *idea* of serving the poor. We simply struggle to accept that our western church model is broken. Most of us, me included, are more committed to sustaining our organizations, be it church or nonprofit, than we are to caring for the vulnerable among us. Our lives are simply too busy to be moved by compassion. When compassion finds its way into our schedule, it is in the form of programmed benevolence. Give away ministry that never asks us to change.

In the beginning, the ministries of presence, listening, serving, and development will forge more change in us than in those around us. This is a natural part of the process of becoming like Christ. The church that makes this kind of transformational commitment to a neighborhood will see God work in amazing ways to bring about reconciliation that reaches well beyond the walls of the church building. Whole blocks become transformed by the work of a renewing gospel.

Bibliography

Gordon, Wayne. *Making Neighborhoods Whole: A Handbook for Christian Community Development*. Downers Grove, IL: InterVarsity, 2013.

Lupton, Bob. *Toxic Charity: How Churches and Charities Hurt Those They Help, And How to Reverse It*. New York: HarperCollins, 2011.

— Chapter 4 —

Backyard Eucharist
The Practice of Neighboring and the Missional Imagination

Shawn Duncan

Giving up on My Calling

For months we prayed, searched endlessly online, and drove countless miles shopping for a house. With each one we prayed: "God, place us where you want us to be. Let us be a part of your mission in the world. Show us where to practice incarnation, where we can be your presence to this broken world." After dozens of visits and two failed contracts, we had finally found the place where we'd raise a family, put down roots, and live into our calling.

It was Easter of 2007 when we moved into the neighborhood. Our weary truck tiptoed up the cracked driveway ducking beneath untrimmed branches and squeezing between unkempt bushes. This faded, old vessel arrived carrying fresh, vibrant dreams of missional possibilities. The answer to our prayers was a ranch-style home with chipped paint, overgrown weeds, and an unending supply of poison ivy. All the proof we needed that

33

this was God's work was the fact that the family next door were Serbian refugees.

God did not even let us get the truck fully unloaded before God's mission for us began. After unloading the washer and dryer, I looked into our neighbors' backyard to see them huddled around a smoking pit outlined by a two-foot high rusted corrugated iron barrier. I looked over at this family God had put us on mission to love and serve, smiled a big friendly, Christianly smile, and waved—ineffectively masking my curiosity at what they could possibly be doing. Without hesitation and in unison they smiled big, hospitable smiles and waved me over—uninterested in masking their welcome to the stranger moving in next door.

Trying to start off on the right missional foot, I jumped the chain link fence between our yards to join them. I was, frankly, more eager to know what was inside the smoking pit than I was to meet our neighbors. I tried to approach casually, as if this were normal for me. I also tried to not look shocked when I peeked over the makeshift wall. My "play it cool" plan was disrupted by the sight of a full lamb, dead and skinned, run through with a spit, being slowly rotated by a homemade rotisserie device over a bed of coals. In their backyard. I tried to look delighted and impressed rather than horrified by the sight of a full lamb being roasted right in front of me. I didn't have a lot of time to control or overcome my shock because their instinctive generosity had deployed the family in serving me some of their bounty. The father leaned over the wall and in one quick motion ripped a leg off the lamb. Before I had time to process the sound of crunch and tear, his son handed me a paper towel with which to hold and eat the leg. The mother and daughter scurried inside returning with fresh, fluffy bread made from scratch and bitter, biting beer imported from Eastern Europe.

That very moment, standing there with backyard Eucharist in hand, was the beginning of the end of my well-formed theology of incarnation. After five years of being neighbored by the Novaks, I gave up my calling to "move into the neighborhood" and to "be Jesus to the least of these." It was in this context of personal and theological disruption The Neighboring Initiative was born.

Researching Neighbors and Neighborhoods

The Neighboring Initiative (TNI) started as a collaborative research project among four colleagues, all of whom worked with nonprofits that equip churches for mission.[1] The co-founders of TNI shared a desire, both professionally and personally, to create space for dynamic learning around challenges many of our friends and colleagues were facing. We were a part of an informal network in Metro Atlanta who had responded to a call to be a neighbor in places where we are out of our racial, religious, and/or socioeconomic comfort zones. For some this meant being in a neighborhood with people of one's own race but where significant poverty was present. For some it meant being white and relocating to a historically African American neighborhood. For others it meant staying put in a transitioning community where more and more refugees and immigrants were filling the schools, subdivisions, and marketplace. Whatever it looked like, we were all living into a call to take up residence among the "last, least, and the lost."

For the first year the TNI team gathered monthly to explore distinct neighborhoods throughout Atlanta. We sat at the feet of longtime residents to understand what it means to join our lives with the lives of neighbors for the sake of the kingdom. We were disrupted, inspired, brought to repentance, and welcomed into the divine beauty of each place. With each visit we identified essential lenses through which one must see their neighbors and neighborhoods if one wants to practice healthy and holistic neighboring.

These immersive encounters and the meetings that followed led TNI to develop a robust philosophy and transformational pedagogy for missional formation. We have seen with painstaking clarity that, no matter how pervasive the language of "missional" is in the North American church, most of what we are doing appears to simply be "mission-ish."

When I Learned I Was a Mission-ish Christian

The new paint on the old walls in our house barely had time to dry before the energy of our missional dreams began to fizzle into guilt and frustration.

We came home from our little Easter BBQ experience barely able to contain the laughter at how God had obviously answered our prayers. We prayed to be the presence of Jesus to a broken world and God moved us in next to refugees, who by our account were desperate people, oppressed by the world's powers, displaced with nowhere to belong. Not only that, these were refugees who cooked *whole animals* over coals in their backyard! We were ready to be the hands and feet of Jesus to this struggling family.

1. Dan Crain, formerly with Polis Institute, now with REMERGE; Shawn Duncan with EIRO; and John and Katheryn Heinz with CenterForm.

Our firstborn son was sixteen months old when we became the neighbors of the Novaks. From that first day they found as many ways as possible to love on our young family. Every time we came home they were sitting on their porch, waving warmly, inviting us to come over, and, through broken English, sit down and talk about life. After a year our family added another little boy, and their generosity grew as well. By the time the boys were walking, they knew exactly where in the Novaks' home to go for a free and endless supply of fresh fruit (and how to easily get ice cream before dinner).

This "desperate, oppressed, displaced" family seemed to have an endless capacity to extend hospitality. Our ability to receive it, however, dried up quickly. To our dismay, we discovered that this family of refugees did not need anything from us. They didn't need us to serve them, provide for them, teach them, or to "be on mission" when we were with them. They just wanted to love us and be loved by us. In short, they wanted to be neighbors. When the dynamics of privilege that were so deeply embedded into our missional imagination were gone and we were left with nothing but the equal footing of being neighbors, we ran out of interest. Before long their instinctive hospitality became a burden to us.

We began this journey praying for open doors for mission, but after one year we were praying the Novaks would not be outdoors so that we could go indoors to be left alone to watch TV. We said we wanted a lifestyle holistically integrated in the mission of God, but what we were living was nothing more than "mission-ish"—a transactional encounter with someone in need, not the mutual transformation of neighboring.[2] We wanted to "serve others" in ways that suited us, that were convenient to us, that were on our terms, and that clearly left us in the role of provider.

I wish I could report that these painful realizations dawned on us quickly and we instantly made the necessary adjustments. In truth, it took us five years before we started articulating our dis-ease. And, unfortunately, it was about that time that a For Sale sign appeared in the Novaks' yard. We begged them to stay, but the needed repairs to their home were too extensive. This unexpected change created an existential crisis, a soul searching that forced us to examine why we had done so poorly at neighboring. God had provided perhaps the easiest family in the world with whom to learn how to be neighbors, but we had failed because of a faulty missional paradigm. We began to see anew the wisdom of Jesus' missional charge in Luke 10 that sent the disciples with no resources whatsoever into neighborhoods

2. Duncan, "3 Questions to Determine if You are Missional or Mission-ish."

to receive and be dependent upon the hospitality of strangers. We were seeing how we did not possess the essential missional competencies of accepting hospitality and experiencing mutuality.

As we grieved the missed opportunity, our eyes were opened to the fact that God put us next door to the Novaks to address our brokenness, not theirs. We confessed and repented of a pride that caused us to miss out on the depths of the blessing in knowing and being known by this family.

When the Sharma family, who are Nepalese refugees, moved into the Novaks' old home, we knew that we were being given a divine do-over. God was inviting us to try for the first time what it might be like to experience kinship, the beauty of the mutual transformation that neighboring can bring.

An Inversion of Incarnational Theology

Thankfully, we were not alone in our need for repentance. Many of our TNI friends could recount very similar disruptive realizations while trying to live incarnationally. It was clear from the beginning that collective expertise was not what drew TNI together; it was a sincere ache for a better way.

Every TNI gathering came with another disruptive idea that required us to reframe our vision for God's mission and how to get caught up within it. The most important theological inversion we experienced, though, was in our understanding of incarnation.

Everyone in TNI had been inspired by the notion that incarnation was more than a doctrine about Jesus; it was a missional call for the church. The call we had received was, "Just as God put on flesh and moved into the neighborhood, we had to put flesh on Jesus' love for the poor and oppressed by moving in next door to them."

As transformative as this teaching was for us, we found that there were inherent power dynamics in that claim that hindered authentic engagement with our neighbors. In this appropriation of the doctrine of incarnation, I was asked to see myself—the white, male, educated, wealthy, lifelong American citizen—as Jesus, and to see my neighbors, conversely, as the dark world into which the light of my goodness would shine. In short, TNI folks had moved in so that they could *be* Jesus. We, however, found that Jesus was already there, and we were being confronted with the challenge of simply *being with* Jesus as he revealed himself in our neighbors.

It was this dramatic inversion of our understanding of incarnation that lead to what is the most foundational principle for any individual or church interested in neighboring: *Incarnation means that Jesus has already moved into your neighborhood. Our call is to discover what he is up to, and ask permission to join him.*

This great inversion opened us up to see that a healthy and holistic approach to neighboring requires an embodied and integrative approach to discipleship, spirituality, and mission.

Jesus as a Six-Year-Old Hindu Girl

After flunking out the first go round, God re-enrolled us in neighboring school under the tutelage of a six year old named Shanti.

She is the youngest member of the Sharma family and is between the ages of our boys. God's gentle prodding into a new way of life was embodied in her light, almost apologetic knock when she'd come over to play. At first, it seemed sweet that she wanted to come over. Before long, though, we had to confront our instinctive annoyance at the sound of a knock at the door or a ring of the doorbell. We saw our home as a retreat from the world, not a place where the sacrament of hospitality could be extended. With persistence Jesus, in the form of a first-grade Hindu girl, tore down our barriers and taught us how to welcome and love our neighbors for the gift that they are to us. She forced us, for the first time in our lives, to make good on the promise of welcome emblazoned on the mat outside our front door.

The challenge of extending welcome to one little girl was far outmatched by receiving the welcome of her whole family, which, for them, means every person from Nepal or Bhutan they may or may not be technically related to within a ten-mile radius of their home.

With hot tea, spicy noodles, colorful decor, a bounteous garden, constant festivals, and, mostly, their genuine, unassuming welcome, the Sharmas have made us one of their own. When they celebrate familial rituals where the generations exchange blessings, we are brought into their living room, given abundant plates of "culture food," sprinkled with rice and anointed with a tikka. In this space, we are not missionaries. We are son, daughter, father, mother, brother, sister. We are family. We belong to one another.

The Sharmas have discipled us in ways the church and seminary never tried and equipped us to walk more fully in the way of Jesus. My wife and I were raised being taught how to do missions, but never learned the ancient art of hospitality. We learned how to lead service projects to meet the needs of the less fortunate, but had not learned how to be served a meal at the table of a stranger. We had learned a desire to change the world, but had not learned to submit to our own transformation at the feet of neighbors. The Sharmas prepared us for the work of loving and being loved by welcoming and being welcomed by neighbors that would come to us from the Caribbean, Middle East, deep American South, Latin America, and beyond. We are learning what it means to submit to God's transformative work as he seeks to draw us into participation with the Spirit and others, revealing the kingdom "on earth as it is in heaven."

The Ethos of The Neighboring Initiative

There are three foundational affirmations that give TNI its theological and pedagogical ethos. First, God is already at work in the places where we live, work, and play (John 5:17). Though it is popular rhetoric for churches to say their mission is to "Bring the kingdom to the city," we are convinced that this is not, nor has it ever been, our call or responsibility. This language of "bringing" represents the genetic code of colonialism, not the gospel. When we examine the verbs that Jesus uses in connection to kingdom, we do not find the disciples being told, despite current missiological parlance, to do any bringing, building, or establishing. The kingdom was not an object under their control, a resource for them to distribute. The kingdom was outside them, beyond them, other than them. They were asked to pursue it, notice it, meditate on it, announce it, and participate in it. This means for us that Jesus moved in long before we did and will remain long after we leave.

Likewise, the parable of the Sheep and Goats does not invite us to go and "be like Jesus to the least of these."[3] This text instead says that Jesus is identified fully with the least of these. If the faulty analogy were true—that the poor were least and we were Jesus—Matthew's text would be nothing more than a stamp of approval on our imperial spirituality.[4] When missions is co-opted this way, the "least-ness" of the poor is exploited and our magnanimity is celebrated. I believe, however, that this parable subverts this power dynamic by saying that Jesus is fully identified with those whom the empire categorizes as invisible, unknowable, disposable. The parable

3. See Audio Adrenaline, "Kings and Queens."
4. Leddy, *The Other Face of God*, 44.

cultivates a contemplative posture so that we can go out to *greet* Jesus, not to *be* Jesus.

Our second affirmation is that the church must deal contextually with the most significant missional prayer in Scripture—the Lord's Prayer or the Our Father. At its center the prayer says, "Your kingdom come on earth as it is in heaven." If that prayer is to have any substance at all, then the "on earth" part means we must live embodied, emplaced lives.[5] For a season my wife and I had committed to praying lauds (morning prayer) together from a small table on our front porch. When we would get to the Our Father, we'd pause at "on earth" and pray for our actual piece of earth—the people on our street, by name, one house at a time. This began to open our hearts to the sacred stirrings happening in the dirt and weeds, mailboxes and shrubs, neighbors and backyards all around us. "On earth" ceased to create a generic globe-like image in our minds and started to look like the quotidian rhythms of the street on which we lived.

Through contextualizing experiments like this, TNI was discovering that the church is in desperate need for a missional renewal that is only possible through a place-based theology.[6] This renewal of mind, spirit, and practice was going to require a new way of praying, a new way of seeing, a new way of being. This leads to TNI's third affirmation—the need for an embodied model for missional formation. Before more is said about that, we need to take a moment to name the great cataract in the missional vision of North American church—*place*.

The Church Needs to Be Re-Placed

As I drive my favorite route from my home to the heart of the city, I pass a major intersection where rapid redevelopment is bringing a parking garage, an organic grocery store, and a variety of other retail and business centers. This bustling intersection was once dominated by the regal presence of one of the area's most historic and prominent congregations. The face of the church building looked unblinking at the convergence of all these streets, the steeple stood towering over all that happened there. It seemed that this church would have an unending and unassailable presence in the city. Week after week, though, I witnessed the grounds get overgrown, the building go up for sale, the sign come down, the boards go up on the windows, the walls

5. Bartholomew, *Where Mortals Dwell*, 2–3.
6. See Brueggemann, *The Land*, and Hjalmarson, *No Home Like Place*.

get knocked in, until all that stood amidst the rubble was a front porch and steeple. For a few days the demolition crew left it standing there, a cross-crowned tower over doors that opened into nothing—nothing except land covered in the broken remains of a church that was being replaced. This towering symbol of Christian influence was given the opportunity to stand fragile, tall, and silent to offer with its haunting presence a final sermon to her sister churches, "Get re-placed or be replaced."

This church told the tale, much like many other congregations in our city, of a bygone era of bursting-at-the-seams growth, significant influence in the community, and the exciting expansion of their campus and minis-tries. The rapid and radical demographic changes in the city, however, led to imperceptible disinvestment from the local community, over-investment in its own preservation, gradual decline, and, eventually, past the place where survival was possible.

This is why TNI exists—to re-place the church. We want to participate in the gospel work of reconciliation, and we believe that the local church is God's intended instrument for that reconciliation. But if the church is going to live fully into that purpose, they have got to reframe their position and posture in the cities in which they find themselves. They need to get re-placed.

The journey to getting re-placed, though, will not be traversed by dou-bling down on the old silo paradigms of mission, spirituality, and disciple-ship that have been, in part, responsible for creating a non-placed church. Re-placement will require a distinctly different approach to discipleship, which brings us back to TNI's third core affirmation—the necessity of an embodied curriculum for missional formation.[7]

The Need for a New Spiritual Formation Model

This call to neighboring is not something that can be solved with new programs, new events, or a new sermon series. We are convinced—based on research and the rugged, lived experience of our friends, mentors, and colleagues—that the call to neighboring is a matter of spiritual formation.

My doctoral research project focused on the factors that influence people to live robust missional lifestyles. I surveyed Christians across the country who were committed to certain missional values and practices. I used the results of these surveys to interview at length fifteen individuals

7. Duncan, "Embodied Curriculum for the Formation of Missional Identity."

who spent significant years in this way of life. The bad news from this research is that the vast majority—88 percent—said that the church had little to nothing to do with leading them to this way of life. This begged the question: What is it that forms people to live holistically missional lives? I discovered a number of fascinating factors that are part of what forms a core pedagogical framework for how missional formation happens. These findings have been combined with the research and expertise of the rest of the TNI leadership team to shape a spiritual formation model that can re-place the church. TNI's embodied discipleship paradigm is defined by:

- Experimentation—The frontiers of neighboring will not be discovered by following well-drawn maps, or trusting in the already-knowns. Only a process of experimentation, trial, failure, confession, and discovery can open us up to missional living.

- Disruption—The most important work of missional formation will not be what we build out there in the neighborhood but what is torn down in us. Our pride, assumptions, and resistance to the other will need to be disrupted before we are able to participate fully in the art of neighboring.

- Immersion—The safe confines of classrooms, the orderliness of off-the-shelf curriculum, and the trusted scholarship of experts are not enough. These traditional approaches may, actually, only reinforce our disembedded, disconnected lives. A new formation model requires the neighborhood to be the school, our neighbors to be the teachers, and the world in which God is working to be the subject.

- Invitation—Missional formation happens in places where the stranger welcomes us in. It is not about going to places we choose for projects we decide to accomplish. It happens when/if/as we are invited by the stranger to walk with her in her world.

- Encounter—Until an authentic encounter, defined by the ability to witness the sacred image of God upon our neighbor, happens, missional formation will not progress. Our ideals about our own triumphant success for God in the world is missionally deformative. When we can finally greet Jesus in our neighbor and submit to his instruction there, then the missional formation process can begin.

The Multidimensional Nature of Neighboring

I have shared just a few (of many) anecdotes of my own failure to love my literal next-door neighbors. As important as it is to build a personal relationship with a neighbor, TNI believes that these interpersonal relationships are but one dimension (we have identified six total) of a healthy and holistic approach to neighboring. Space does not allow me to share our journey of neighboring through the other five dimensions. We have just as many stories of failure and delight from learning to love our neighbor-*hood*—the schools, businesses, civic entities, government agencies, and the other 30,000 people that make up our pocket of Metro Atlanta.

To provide a basic framework for holistic neighboring, TNI has identified these six core dimensions:

- Neighbor to Neighbor—This is the interpersonal work. People with people. Life to life. Not just among individuals but people groups learning to love and embrace other people groups.

- Neighbor to Place—This is about learning to love, think theologically about, and to engage the built environment, the institutions, the history, and the cultures that make up a particular place.

- Neighbor to Church—The church in your neighborhood is essential to neighboring well. It is about partnering with them in pursuit of the kingdom on your shared piece of earth.

- Neighbor to Systems—In every place there are systems of power—corrosive and redemptive, formal and informal. These systems are economic, interpersonal, religious, governmental, and cultural. Neighboring means learning to engage (redemptively or subversively) with the forces that form (or deform) life in your neighborhood.

- Neighbor to God—The North American church has unfortunately crafted a sense that our spiritual practices "recharge" our batteries so we can go into the world to be "emptied out" in mission. TNI abandons this for a "spirituality of the road."[8] If God is out in the world working ahead of us, missional living is a spiritual encounter. God is the first neighbor. Neighboring is first and foremost an intimate participation with God.

---

8. Bosch, *A Spirituality of the Road*.

- Neighbor to Self—Neighboring well includes celebrating your own personhood and delight, indulging curiosities, enjoying hobbies. Your neighborhood doesn't need a worn-out, spent-up martyr for the cause. Your neighborhood needs you to be a person fully alive to life.

The call to join God in the reconciliation of all things means living whole lives that are wholly caught up in the whole life of a particular place. This eschatological vision only has texture and traction when it is brought to bear in very specific places among very specific people. To do this, though, we have to go beyond trying to meet needs and start seeking reconciled community.

The Epicenter for Reconciliation

The missional cataract of our placelessness has blurred our ability to see a more robust telos of why the North American church does mission, outreach, or benevolence. Regardless of the program or its results, most of what we are doing aims at objectives far too paltry for a gospel-centered people. I often ask groups, "If your ministry perfectly reached its goal, what would that look like?" If it is building schools in Ghana, they could say, "Every child in Ghana has a school to attend." If it is distributing food to low-income children in the summer, they could say, "Every child in our city has all the food they need during the summer."

These, of course, are admirable goals. They are, however, insufficient. The gospel's end game is not ensuring that people who do not have enough stuff have enough stuff. Jesus' kingdom is not a world of independently wealthy individuals not depending upon anyone else for anything else. The eschatological end of the gospel is *reconciled community*. The end of the gospel is not materialistic; it is eucharistic. The fulfilled vision of the kingdom is the new humanity. Despite this, it is rare in the midst of our school-building, food-distributing, shelter-providing to see people at the table with one another. Our missional cataract prevents us from asking: "Are we seeing the housed family and the family facing homelessness joining lives? Are we seeing the low-income kids and the kids living in affluence playing at birthday parties together? Are we seeing those living in western abundance and the displaced peoples from the developing world entering into communion together?" The gospel is about reconciled community, not distributing physical goods. And the epicenter for reconciliation is the practice of neighboring.

If we are not interested in joining lives at the neighborhood level, then there is little potential that we can realize the beloved community at a systemic level. Neighboring, we believe, is both the means and the end of a truly gospel-centered, kingdom-pursuing people.

Don't misunderstand me. God is unequivocally concerned with the hungry being fed, children being educated, the homeless housed. We are required by God to ensure people have the physical resources needed to thrive. I am not promoting a soul-saving, noncorporeal gospel. Shared material resources ought to be emerging out of the context of authentic community, not programs that, in many ways, only serve to prop up and justify our distance from one another.

Unfortunately, however, the North American church is suffering from a proximity disorder, the geographic and relational distance that prevents the expression and experience of authentic mission, discipleship, and spirituality. Until we address this disorder, we will not be able to live into the eschatological vision of God for a reconciled community. We have been grateful to have our own lives disrupted, and we are inviting you to invert your understanding of incarnation, develop a contemplative approach to your neighborhood, and learn how to experience the mutual transformation of hospitality.

Come to the Table

As a spiritual practice to help us live into our neighboring skin, my family has worked with our neighbors to throw a few block parties. Games in the street for the kids, tables for conversation for the adults, and lots of food and drink for everyone. I will never forget one spring Saturday when we were all gathered in our neighbor's yard talking, laughing, playing, and feasting together. There was a moment when the realization struck that I was experiencing a foretaste of the kingdom. There were white and black southerners, immigrants from Nepal, Pakistan, Jamaica, and Honduras, all gathered together to fill these folding chairs and picnic tables with a vision of the world to come. "I say to you many will come from the East and the West and will take their place at the feast with Abraham, Isaac, and Jacob in the Kingdom of heaven" (Matt 8:11).

Bibliography

Audio Adrenaline. "Kings and Queens." http://audioa.com/lyrics.

Bartholomew, Craig G. *Where Mortals Dwell: A Christian View of Place for Today.* Grand Rapids: Baker Academic, 2015.

Bosch, David. *A Spirituality of the Road.* Eugene, OR: Wipf and Stock, 2001.

Brueggemann, Walter. *The Land: Place as Gift, Promise, and Challenge in Biblical Faith.* Minneapolis: Fortress, 1989.

Duncan, Shawn. "Embodied Curriculum for the Formation of Missional Identity: What Liminal Churches Can Learn From Practitioners of Christian Community Development." DMin diss., Columbia Theological Seminary, 2014.

_____. "3 Questions to Determine if You are Missional or Mission-ish." http://themissionalnetwork.com/who/your-story/3-questions/.

Hjalmarson, Leonard. *No Home Like Place: A Christian Theology of Place.* Portland, OR: Urban Loft, 2015.

Leddy, Mary Jo. *The Other Face of God: When the Stranger Calls Us Home.* Maryknoll, NY: Orbis, 2011.

— Chapter 5 —

Dwelling in Union
Asset-Based Community Development

Catherine Gilliard

Once rich and thriving, the English Avenue neighborhood of Atlanta, my community, was systemically stripped of sustainable resources and anchors, thereby ensuring that it could no longer provide the quality of life desired by its residents. Over time, neighborhoods like ours that have been stripped of sustainable resources eventually develop negative reputations for being unsafe and undesirable places to live. Then, dismantled and left for years to deteriorate, they become an economic incentive for external investors and developers. For English Avenue, the economic incentive was the expansion largely through both surrounding property acquisition of universities and the construction of a new sports stadium for Atlanta. Abandoned houses creating blight combined with reduced community services by the city also created a perfect storm for external agencies to bring "compassionate" solutions that were not requested, desired, or invited by resident engagement or affirmation.

Asset-based community development (ABCD) has become a best practice process for the development of under-resourced communities. Typical implementation uses resources like asset mapping, soliciting community input, enlisting gifts, inviting participation, grassroots community organizing, and intentional collaboration. These methods are effectively used by external agencies and individuals who are moved by compassion, or driven by profit. The evaluation of developmental effectiveness is in the ability of the planners to restore each community to a place of sustainability. Research focused on the drivers that turn blighted neighborhoods into thriving and flourishing communities shape the foundational methods of ABCD strategies.

Believers in Christ have a role in shaping the approach and implementation of ABCD strategies. Believers are called by a biblical mandate, not a worldview motivated by economic profit, to reclaim God's vision for the city. Each community's journey of restoration is unique and provides another opportunity for God's story of provision, care, and nurture to emerge. Our experience, as a local church using ABCD strategies, is based on building relationships as neighbors in ways that demonstrate God's love for those who have been marginalized and forgotten by our society. The word *community* has a compound meaning: "com"—meaning "with"—and "unity"—meaning "to dwell in union." Believers are called to dwell in union with our neighbors.

An ABCD approach differs from a needs-based approach where external agencies, organizations and individuals, determine what problems exist in an under-resourced community. Community development is approached by identifying deficiencies, needs, and problems. Those who begin with this orientation soon begin to conduct research that asks what is wrong in this community and with the people who live in it. Social service agencies, nonprofits, government, and businesses begin community development by addressing what needs to be fixed and what needs to change. Residents are contacted to be subjects in surveys, providing data for outside agencies to determine which problems need to be addressed. Organizers mobilize support to solve identified problems from the outside. At the heart of this approach is the belief that residents are not capable of solving their own problems.

Those who practice ABCD begin with knowing that every community has assets: the residents have gifts, and the community can form a development plan based upon their strengths, gifts, and vision. It is the call of the community church to extend these truths into practice in the neighborhoods in which they are called to serve. God loves the poor, the outcast, the marginalized, those who suffer, and all who are oppressed and rejected. Jesus demonstrated God's love for all who are oppressed and rejected by coming from heaven in human form to intentionally live among them, fellowship with them, deliver them, and heal them. As disciples, we are called to do the same for others. Our strategy begins with loving and living among those on the margins.

Several members of our church have relocated into the English Avenue community motivated by Jesus' example. Members of our congregation relocated not to advocate on behalf of others, but to be one with others. Our struggle against systemic injustice should be a collective response as neighbors who struggle with those we are "dwelling and have union with." We believe Jesus modeled being one with those who are suffering, marginalized, and outcast as he traveled from community to community. Therefore, those members who move should not focus on fixing anything, or addressing problems, but rather be present in obedience to our call to live among those who are suffering, just as Jesus modeled for us.

After twenty years of being in the community, we have discovered how the church and outside agencies and individuals struggle with unconscious biases, or blind spots, in how we think about and perceive other people. Unconscious biases are beliefs and attitudes that affect the way we look at, encounter, respond to, and make sense of the world around us. These biases become our pattern for decision-making about others, based on what we believe feels safe, familiar, and valuable, without consciously realizing we are making these judgments. Unconscious biases divide communities into categories of "us" and "them," often creating suspicion about our intentions and our process for community development. These biases happen automatically, and often reveal deep-seated prejudices and stereotypes, as our brains are triggered to make judgments and assessments of people and situations, influenced by our own familial background, cultural environment, and personal experiences. Without a process for developing an awareness of these biases, our process for community development will only confirm for residents the suspicion that those who are mobilizing are not interested in the contextual values that already exist among the residents of the community.

The local church advocates on behalf of residents by communicating with outside agencies and individuals about the need for an ABCD approach through the facilitation of intentional neighboring. In our church we began a regular series of open conversations on race, gender, power, and gentrification in order to help name the fears of residents and the long history of broken promises made to them. We invited long-term residents, church members, and those who were entering into the community to be a part of understanding the underlying emotions that are present whenever someone (or something new) enters into the neighborhood with a new plan for development.

Underlying these emotions is a host of fears including: the fear of losing power, fear of the unknown, fear of undermining credibility, fear of our own ignorance, fear of how people will come in and change the way we do things around here, and the fear of being displaced as neighborhood decisions are being made by those who don't live in the community, but seek to profit from the assets present in it. If we are to be long-term residents in under-resourced communities, we must name these fears and the unconscious biases we hold. A local church can host communal conversations where the naming of fears and suspicions and the awareness of the unconscious biases that are present, help those who will form collaborative networks to reach a deeper understanding of where the emotions stem from and how new seeds can be planted for new attitudes, behaviors, and partnerships to form through intentional neighboring.

For members of our congregation, that meant a long-term commitment of intentional neighboring, where generations of neighbors build relationships, share life, and learn to address complex social issues. Intentional neighboring believes relationships go beyond living next door to one another. More so, caring and nurturing relationships grow out of a general concern for one another and for those who are vulnerable in our community. Residents view one another as friends who go through trauma, change, transition, and celebration while deepening their dependence upon social capital.

Social capital is based on the theory that social networks have value. Social capital refers to the collective value of who people know and how pre-established relationships impact expectations of reciprocity and interdependence. Social capital emphasizes a wide variety of specific benefits that flow from the trust, reciprocity, information, and cooperation associated with being a part of a social network. Social capital creates value both for and in the people who are connected in exchange for services and resources that are normally provided through financial capital.

For English Avenue residents, understanding the intersectionality and complexity of social capital meant naming and addressing the intricate issues of racial and economic diversity. Members of our congregation, who moved into the community, had to learn how to trust the long-term residents who lived there, and become students in understanding the contours of the racial and economic divide present in communities undergoing gentrification in order to move the process towards ABCD.

Gentrification is a negative word in under-resourced communities. It is defined as a process of renewal and rebuilding of deteriorating areas, accompanying the influx of middle-class or affluent people, who displace poorer residents. Historically, it uses the process of buying and renovating houses, stores, apartments, and other properties in deteriorated urban neighborhoods to improve property values, with the result of displacing low-income families and small businesses. Gentrification is an issue of class and privilege. The goal of gentrification is not improving an area, but the displacement of certain people from it.

Gentrification is not about bringing essential resources to a community that desperately needs it, it's about stealing the necessities of the underclass to fund and further the privileged class. Gentrification is not about raising property value, it's about forcing historically rent-driven citizens out of their homes, with prices beyond their incomes, so current residents can no longer afford to reside in their own community. To put it simply, gentrification is modern-day colonialism.

Colonialism is the practice of acquiring control over another country, occupying it with settlers and exploiting it for economic gain. Through the practice of gentrification, "those who acquire control," or the ruling class, are the external agencies, the "country" becomes the neighborhood, the "settlers" become those moving in, and the "exploitation for economic gain" is the process of displacement of long-term residents. What is evident in many communities undergoing development is the unconscious biases that have deep roots in colonialism. Colonialism is embedded in our history as a nation and rings hollow with residents who become those who will be exploited for economic gain. When the ruling class wants the resources of the country it is taking over, they also want to use the indigenous people as labor. In the beginning of these practices, the majority native population is being exploited by a minority class. The ruling class is always a minority when colonialism begins. The process continues as the ruling class takes more and more of the resources to feed its empire. Where this gets complicated for the ruling class is when other ruling classes have competing and overlapping colonial projects, oftentimes on the same turf, and more than one group comes and makes claims to the same land, all without regard to the native population, who would simply prefer to be left alone.

Today, in community development, we see this colonialism model played out when external groups practice the *"savior"* complex, or use the "let's help those poor people" approach. Today, the new colonialism is called development, and is again driven by those who see economic advantage through gentrification and acquisition of desired parcels of property. The "fixing" of community problems is decided by outside groups who often have interest in personal and corporate economic gain. Moved by profit, the goal becomes to make the neighborhood more desirable for future investors and higher-income residents. Once a forgotten community, these neighborhoods become valuable assets again, usually because location, businesses, organizations, and individuals will be in competition to provide the most "needed" services and competing resources that current residents may have neither asked for nor desire. A mistaken and all-too-common approach to development is for external agencies to present plans for growth without building upon appreciative inquiry or social capital.

In communal conversations our church studied and named how the process of power and control connected the dots between gentrification and colonization. In gentrification, the community has been stripped of community assets through closure and relocation of resources. Once a community has been targeted by the ruling class for gentrification, a very important part of the process is to create disorientation for the current residents through renaming the community and the streets that identify its location for the larger metro community. In our neighborhood the streets were renamed and reprinted on large green street signs while the streets known by the current residents became very small black-and-white signs with the word *historic* in front of the old name. In community meetings you hear the confusion when developers use the new names of the streets and residents ask the question, "Where?" and someone explains, "The old . . . ," using the boundary names that current residents are familiar with.

Our local church began to speak about the importance of keeping the historic legacy of our community alive by naming the neighborhood community garden after a long-term resident who passed away. Keeping historical markers and memories alive connects current residents to their rich history as a community and adds value to the contextual ways in which moving forward can build on those examples, rather than erasing them from our memories.

Believers who hold a kingdom vision of community approach ABCD by valuing and mobilizing individual and community assets through appreciative inquiry relationships. Appreciative inquiry listens to the voices of residents in the community to embrace, understand, and analyze what has meaning and would be considered a successful development of their neighborhood. To begin by listening and understanding contextual values, the development process communicates and strengthens the confidence of the residents that whatever upcoming strategies are being planned will use their skills and capacities in collaborative approaches to development.

In under-resourced communities with rich histories, older residents can remember the days when their community flourished and when it came together in times of tragedy and pain. They recall days when the elderly in their community were honored, respected, and felt protected. Retirees can share the stories of the people who guided them and those who betrayed them. Their stories include important information about the history of the neighborhood, but also about the shared values that were a part of the community's DNA. Our members, who moved into the neighborhood, found this to be the place where residents were most truthful about personal stigmatization, historical and present challenges, and their vision for their neighborhood renewal.

The youth of our church participated in a project of collecting the oral histories of residents that had lived in the community for a long time. A member of our church contacted StoryCorps, which is housed at the Atlanta History Center, to train our youth in how to conduct an interview, phrase questions, and record the interviews in ways that allowed their conversation to flow. We hoped that through this process, our youth and older adults would come together for an intergenerational conversation, sharing the stories of what life in their community used to look like, the struggles that the community came together to address, and the hopes that older residents had for the future of their community.

The local church believes the Holy Spirit equips female and male, old and young, disabled and able-bodied people from every ethnicity, culture, and tribe with varying spiritual gifts. These gifts are to be used to build up the entire community. Believers are called to recognize the gifts of others and to provide opportunities for others to grow in their gifts. This recognition must be at the heart of ABCD. We build diverse relationships within under-resourced communities while being very aware that we must not segregate along lines of age, race, household income, or ability. It is important for shared core values to be embraced by all who are residents and those who will become residents of the community.

The students in our after school program gave a community presentation on "The History of English Avenue." Photographs of the community from years past through today surrounded the sanctuary and our students conducted research on the people who had streets named after them in our community, famous and influential people who had grown up in our community, and the long-term resident for whom our community garden/green space was named.

Another project that engaged the gifts of our youth was the design and production of our neighborhood mural. A local artist was hired to depict a peaceful scene of diverse children playing together and our youth worked with the artist to bring the concept to life. Their creative skills were enhanced as they worked alongside the artist to communicate to the community a message of hope, inclusion, and peace.

ABC developers bring to their work a knowledge of the unspoken history that is always present during times of conversation and collaboration, understanding that part of the process of building trust is to release power and control. Consequently, priorities should always be set in collaboration by those most affected by the decision. The determination on how power is shared needs to be defined by those without power, just as the priorities are set by those who have the most to lose. This reversal of power and release of control means that ABCD intentionally slows down the process until those who need more time to understand the changes that are and will be happening challenge, support, reject, or accept the transitions that are ahead.

Our church is a convener of community gatherings. Whether it is sponsoring family movie nights outside on the green—an old dump site that residents and members of our church transitioned into a green space—or for raising awareness and advocacy for issues that are of concern to residents, such as hosting a "reel justice" film festival on mass incarceration, or prayer vigils as a Christian response to mass incarceration, we see our role as peacemakers, making our facility available for conversation, presentations, meetings, and conferences. The church needs to be viewed as a place of connection, inclusion, and hope, as residents struggle with the reality that outside forces are entering in with money, power, and influence. The infusion of these resources often builds unhealthy relationships between organizations, associations, and churches. It is easy to envision how these organizations, who have been starving for resources, would be tempted to align with the plans and programs of those who have the power to shape a new reality for people who are unaware of the profit motives behind the new plans for development.

The development of under-resourced communities should involve the long-term kingdom vision of our being known for our love for one another, demonstrated through our care for one another. An ABCD strategy doesn't enter in asking what is wrong or what needs to be fixed. We begin with the Word of God to frame our context for a kingdom vision of the city or community that has been targeted for development. We begin by asking questions of ourselves, our motives, and our ability to see others as God sees them. Much has been written about the approach of restoring dignity, worth, and value to others in the implementation of ABCD. What I am proposing is that there is much work to be done by those who are the developers before they begin the process of implementing strategies. We have learned that for these strategies to work there must be intentional preparation on the part of those who move in and those who provide the requested resources to neighborhoods undergoing development.

Each community has a God story. ABC developers should focus on the various ways that God's contextual story can be told, protected, and valued. The church should have an active role in the development of the community where she has been called to minister. We are the active witness of God in our community. How we honor those who have been marginalized, how we care for those who need treatment, how we nurture those filled with questions and anger, and how we love those society has named as unlovable redeems the church in the eyes of those who need to see the hope of Christ demonstrated in real and tangible ways.

As the church utilizes faith-rooted methods to mediate between the powers that are driven by profit and not faith, as the church finds her power in the spiritual gifting of the people whom God has drawn into each community, as the church remembers her mission and ministry to love justice, do mercy, and walk humbly with our God, we can see the strategies of ABCD become a powerful process of interpreting and demonstrating the relationship building embodied in intentional neighboring. At the foundation of our beliefs in community development, we believe that everyone is needed and everyone's gifts should be involved and included in the process.

Ultimately, our church has found that it is neither the dreams of the long-term residents nor the visions of those who are moving in that have sustainable power. After twenty years of neighboring, we have found that the sustainable pieces of our community development are those that align with God's vision. In those places where development has provided discipleship mentoring, communal conversations on divisive topics, the sharing of power and resources, and the care for those who are physically, emotionally, or mentally ill, we see God's hand providing the sustainability that each community desires to model.

We believe churches are places where development strategies are lived out. Our congregants who live in the community become image bearers and vision casters of what the kingdom of God looks like when neighbors care for, look out for, and advocate with and for one another. We model how to give voice to the voiceless among us, empower those who have lost hope among us, and encourage awareness of the ways in which the agency of those who are angered and frustrated can be effectively used to address systemic change. Food pantries, clothing ministries, and giveaways are compassion ministries that use available resources to bridge crisis moments. Long-term development strategies focus on the causes of crisis and provide strategic thinking around making sustainable resources available.

Bike repair shops, intramural competitions in sporting and fitness events and on-site giveaways provide youth and those who support them with activities that keep them occupied, but the control and power of these entities still remain in the hands of external agencies who compete for coveted after-school hours. Churches, who prepare their youth for future opportunities, understand the importance of having these moments of fun and play, but also recognize the seriousness of preparation for the competitive encounters facing youth in their futures. Programs that should fall on the weekend are introduced during these afternoon hours in direct conflict with after-school programs because the ruling class is often unwilling to sacrifice their weekends, which are reserved for their own personal agendas. Programs that have long provided mentoring and discipleship are now in direct competition with short-term distractions, thus limiting the future opportunities that are available to youth in under-resourced communities.

When ABCD strategies are at their best, developers are not teaching residents how to fish, or control when they can fish. Developers are sharing information and resources on how residents can own their own pond. The skills that are necessary to equip and empower both adult residents and the youth in an under-resourced community are limited because the internal motives of the developers are often hidden behind the unconscious biases they hold. Our focus shouldn't be on just helping people, but instead sharing what we have learned. Under those circumstances, our neighbors learn from one another how to embrace positive ways to help themselves. True restoration and redemption ministries embody ABCD strategies that ask new questions because of the relationships that are formed and deepened through intentional neighboring.

From poor personal health care that plagues disenfranchised communities, to environmental pollutants often present in under-resourced communities, residents can be trained through awareness on how to effectively mobilize and bring healing resources to their neighborhood through collaboration. It is through ABCD that education, training, and mentoring can form its most powerful relationships. Collaboration with representatives that offer certified and degree-based learning opportunities has proven to be a strategic process for shifting the power dynamics in a community. The church is usually filled with congregants who have this knowledge, training, and the skills necessary to empower a new generation of leaders. However, what the church is usually lacking is the vision and commitment of members to see themselves in these mentoring roles.

Our faith demands more than surface participation in changing the realities of those who have been forgotten, oppressed, and rejected. Through ABCD, the church can redeem the hope of a new generation of leaders who need to see themselves and those they are in relationship with differently. The church is called to model God's love in sacrificial ways, giving all that has been given to us to those in need. Sadly, and all too often, this is communicated in financial terms. We are sent out into the world, ambassadors of an abundant God, with limitless resources, to restore each neighborhood, community, and city to more fully reflect God's love for humanity. The church must see this vision, understand what it means for this vision to unfold, and then willingly submit to being obedient to living it out in relationship with others.

If the struggles that exist in our under-resourced communities are truly dependent upon local churches engaging neighbors as image bearers of God, then the work of ABCD doesn't begin with planning or programming. Instead, we must begin with our hearts being prepared to face the systemic evil that we will address when fighting for justice for all people. In the days of the civil rights movement, nonviolent protestors were trained in churches on how to respond when violent and evil predators would launch their attack on those fighting for equality and justice. It is this type of on the ground, one-on-one training that I believe will bring a new level of effectiveness to our resistance to the model of gentrification that is invading the communities of families who find themselves in places that are now desired by the ruling class. When the church remembers the power of sharing the faith-based resources given to us by the Holy Spirit and the cruciform life we are called to live, then the beauty of community that is desired by all residents is not only a future reality, but one that is sustained through the life-giving, generational models that we learn about, experience, and pass on. Our role, as believers in Christ, is to be actively aware of our own biases as we encounter each evil design, belief, or proclamation that holds people in bondage to suffering, displacement, or oppression for potential profits. Transformation happens through the church being intentional, vulnerable, and confessional. May the Holy Spirit's power continue to shape the church to be transformed into the image of Christ so that all who have a church in their local community will be able to see a witness of a caring God who uses people who call on the Lord to reverse the power of evil in their lives. As the church uses ABCD to help implement strategies for renewal, let's remember to do so with God's kingdom vision in mind.

— Chapter 6 —

Race, Reconciliation, Recognition
A Generational Search for
the Beloved Community

Bruce Aaron Beard and Donell Woodward

Editor's Note: I initially invited Donell to contribute this chapter based on his work with racial reconciliation. He agreed, but suggested that his father, Bruce, who has long been heavily active in the fight for racial reconciliation and justice, join him in the project. Donell works in the historic Sweet Auburn district of Atlanta, which is the birthplace of Dr. Martin Luther King, Jr. and still houses the historic heart of the civil rights movement. Bruce's perspective more closely resonates with what Sweet Auburn historically represents, while Donell represents a building on this historic foundation. Part I of this essay is Bruce's story and contribution. Part II is Donell's.

Part I

The conclusion of the creation story reads, "God saw all that he had made, and behold, it was very good" (Gen 1:31a). This was stated after God had finished the pinnacle of his creation, humans. It pleased God to create us to be the target of his affection, created to be loved by him, to love him in return, and to love each other. The God kind of love makes no distinctions; it's more than a feeling, it is action for the good of others. True love gives sacrificially. John declares, "For God so loved the world, that he gave . . ." (John 3:16). There is no true love apart from giving. But this verse tells of the level of sacrifice love is willing to make: "he gave his only begotten son . . . ." Formed from the love of God, should humans do any less? If we love God, should we not do the same? Unfortunately, history has taught us what happens when this love is lost—we become lovers of self and haters of "others."

It is my belief that our omniscient God created diversity on purpose. Men and women are not the same; ethnicities, cultures, races, and worldviews are not the same. A garden is most beautiful when many colors and types of flowers are present. I'm glad daffodils don't move away to a new garden when tulips are planted close by. It is the beautiful array of humanity, in all their particularities, that brings glory to God. I believe it was God's intention that the uniqueness of humans would build and enhance each other. Like a couple united in marital bliss, though different, becomes one, so it should be with all of humanity.

The sad reality is that the gift of diversity that God had planned for humans to bring him glory and be a great blessing to each other, humans have managed to turn into something that makes angels cry, brings glory to the Evil One, and causes God's highest creation on earth to languish in division, suffering, and despair. My God, what have we done?

A strange feeling swept over me as I approached the Elmina Slave Castle in Ghana, West Africa. The area was beautiful. The view of the clear blue Atlantic waters meeting the sandy beaches was breathtaking. The scene was surreal. There was the beauty of the ocean and a majestic castle, but what happened inside the castle was unimaginably horrible. Standing inside the male dungeon, we heard the story of how millions of Africans had come through this place. Nude, hungry, and cramped into an extremely crowded space with little ventilation and no toilet, many died before reaching the "Door of No Return." As I watched tears fall down the cheeks of visitors from various nations, I felt my own tears begin to fall. It suddenly struck me: if I, an African American, was standing there in that dungeon, it was very possible, if not probable that someone from my family line had been there as a slave . . . and survived.

In the female dungeon we learned that when the Portuguese, Dutch, or British leader of the castle decided he wanted a slave woman, she was chained to a cannon ball in the courtyard until she no longer resisted and was then taken to the "master bedroom" for days or weeks until she was passed along to other staff and then killed. What was perhaps most disturbing was that the female dungeon was under a church in the center of the castle. The inscription above the exit door to the church was from Psalms: "This is my resting place for ever and ever, here I sit enthroned, for I have desired it" (Ps 132:13–14). For over 300 years millions must have seen that inscription on their way to death and/or torture.

While Elmina was one of the earliest such castles along Africa's west coast, in time there would be over thirty. Once passing through the "Door of No Return" most would never see their homes, families, or Africa again. No one knows how many died on the trip here. One ship left West Africa with 594 slaves. When it arrived there were ninety-eight. Estimates range from 30 to 60 million persons died in the trade over 400 years.

In the centuries that have since passed it is clear that there have been two Americas, two worldviews, and two sets of collective experiences. When Thomas Jefferson and the framers of the US Constitution wrote with such eloquence, words conveying the oneness of all people "under God," and espousing "freedom and justice for all," the Africans in America were slaves and those amazing words did not apply to them. Thomas Jefferson inherited over 175 slaves, and by natural increase owned over 600 humans. It took fourteen amendments to the Constitution before African Americans were declared citizens of the United States after nearly 400 years. Adopted on July 9th, 1868, just three years after the Thirteenth Amendment ended slavery, the Fourteenth Amendment promised citizenship rights and equal protection under the law to all.

For most, however, that amendment proved only empty words; the reality was something very different. Initially there was great hope. After centuries of torture, husbands having to watch their wives sexually abused by slave masters and overseers (although formal marriage was prohibited among slaves), children sold away from their mothers, lynchings, and even live slow roasting of slaves, hope had come. After planned rapes by slave owners and their staff resulted in greater diversity of color among the slaves, treating those with lighter complexions more favorably than darker ones created division among the slaves that ensured against plantation uprisings, hope had come. But soon came despair.

The 1900s saw dramatic change and challenges. Black soldiers would fight for America on foreign soil, but in segregated platoons, each with white supervision. When they returned home, there were no jobs for them and they still did not have the right to vote. There were court battles over laws in some states that made teaching black children how to read illegal. There were battles for equal justice and equal treatment under federal and state law. Legal conflicts ensued over hiring and retention practices, admissions to colleges, access to fair housing, and receiving small business loans. And there were the continued battles over policing in black communities. Sadly, now in the twenty-first century many of the same struggles and battles continue.

Why is racial reconciliation so difficult? In addition to being a university professor, I am also a pastor and community activist. I have often been asked to lead conferences, workshops, and speak in churches during Sunday worship to address this issue. I recall one time when a group of white clergy were planning to hold such an event for their congregations. We met for breakfast to discuss the format for the event. I was the only African American present. I noticed Pastor Steve (not his real name) grew very quiet. After a time I asked if he was all right. Somewhat reluctantly he began to speak. He had just realized something he never thought about before. He said he grew up in a white family with white parents. He lived in an all-white community and all his friends were white. He graduated from white schools and attended a predominately white college and had little interaction with the few black students that were there. He earned his degree and went to work at a company whose owners were white with a mostly white staff. For recreation he played on golf courses where blacks were not officially excluded, but he never saw any. He attended a white church and later became the pastor of a white congregation. He said that he didn't think he was a racist but had to admit, he knew nothing about black people, black history, and the struggle of black people. Most of what he learned about blacks was from television. The thing about it was, as he stated it, he never had to think about black people—there was no need for him to know or understand. The plight of blacks was something that had never been a part of his reality. But then he turned to me and looked intently in my eyes and said, "*But you have to live with your blackness in a white world every day, how awful.*" Enlightenment! There was a world going on next to him that he had never seen or considered. That moment of realization, I believe, changed him forever.

The day of the event, I walked out to a crowd of about 500 people. Most there were white, some black, some Latino, and some Asian. At the conclusion, a very astute older white gentleman came up, apparently moved by the day's event. He reached out his hand to me in friendship and said, "You know brother, I don't even notice that you are black." Well, I'm of a light complexion but clearly black. I certainly understood what he meant. He was trying to say that color did not matter to him. However, while I accepted his hand of friendship, I said to him, "*Notice, notice that I am black. To say you don't notice is to say that you cannot see what is unique about me. You dismiss my ancestral story, my own life's journey as a black man in a white world, and most of all what God has intended in making me black. So let's do this: I'll notice you're white and will seek to glean what God intended in your whiteness. You notice my blackness and seek to glean some sense of my ethnic uniqueness. By God's infinite wisdom, we can grow together.*"

If you have ever owned a fishbowl and filled it with various kinds of fish, you know watching them swim can be a calming, relaxing experience. Sometimes they will swim to the glass as if looking straight at you with a smile and a hello. Ever wonder what the fish are experiencing? Maybe they were born and bred in a bowl and have never known what it's like to swim free in open waters. Perhaps there is something, somewhere deep inside the fish that longs for that something they never had, freedom. What if when they swim to the edge of the glass they are hoping the face on the other side has come to take them to a place where they can swim with no glass cell? What if the conditions of the water they were swimming in changed? The water becomes too warm or too cold for their natural survival. Perhaps the chemical composition of the water is out of balance. To the person on the outside the water looks fine, crystal clear, but to the fish, it's a different experience. If that fish peering back at you from the other side of the glass, seemingly content, were in fact screaming for help, would you know? Of course not, we couldn't know what they're experiencing, we can't hear their voice; we are content with our assumptions that the fish are fine when in reality they are dying. We don't recognize their pain because we don't recognize them as one of us. They are a different species and we can only understand them on the basis of our standard, not their very real condition.

If blacks are seen and understood through the lens of white eyes and white experience in America, reconciliation will never be possible. In 1903, W. E. B. Dubois wrote a book titled *The Souls of Black Folk*. In one section he deals with the issue among African Americans that he calls "double consciousness." His premise is that blacks in America are of African origin but were not born in, raised in, and (mostly) have never been in Africa. At the same time blacks are in America, are American citizens, but have never been accepted in whole or in part as equal to whites in America. He argued that blacks are neither fully African nor American and for that reason have had to fight and struggle for identity and simple recognition.

Reconciliation is like when a married couple begins to have difficulty in their marriage. Later they reconcile and come together as one. They began as one and come back together as one. There has never been oneness between the races, so reconciliation on our own, without first recognizing the unique blessing of each as seen through the eyes of our creator God, cannot happen.

The first church where I served as pastor was racially mixed, but had a predominantly black congregation. It was named after a church with a predominantly white congregation. The church was founded in 1865, the year the Emancipation Proclamation was signed into law. I discovered that prior to its founding the original members of the church had been slaves of the members of the white church. Once slavery officially ended and the black church was founded, since blacks could hold no office or title and Virginia law did not permit blacks to congregate without white supervision, the pastor, deacons, and trustees were the same pastor, deacons, and trustees of the white church. The church I served had been named "First Colored Baptist Church." Both congregations at the time belonged to the Southern Baptist Convention. Before changing conventions, I once attended a Southern Baptist session. I was one of very few black pastors. Nearly everyone I met thought that I was on the staff of the white church, serving under the white pastor. Our congregation was not recognized. Recognition must precede reconciliation.

So what does recognition mean? It does not require an intimate knowing of the struggles of blacks in America, but it does require a realizing that the black experience in America is vastly different and cannot be compared to or understood by the standards of the white experience. It's recognizing that when African Americans say "Black Lives Matter," they are not saying other lives don't matter. It simply means that in America, all lives have always seemed to matter except black lives and that of other people of color, like Native Americans who suffered extreme genocide while governmental legislation made it legal. When African Americans protest against police brutality, it's not because blacks don't want the help and protection of the police like everyone else, and it's not because they are not thankful for the help of the police when they receive it. But there is documented, historical evidence that police brutality has been a major problem in many black communities since slavery. It's not that blacks have a problem with predominantly white universities, businesses, banks, schools, etc. It's when there is proven or even subtle discrimination by these institutions that it's problematic. However, many in the white community think the playing field is equal when it never has been. It's the assumption that the criminal justice system is fair to all when there is documented evidence that African Americans are incarcerated at a much higher rate and given much longer sentences on average than others who are convicted of the same offenses.[1] It's the person on the outside of the fishbowl who can't hear the screams of a dying fish inside. It's a man who can't understand his wife's description of the pain she feels in childbirth. It's telling a rape victim that somehow it's her fault. The experiences may be different but they are real. They may be hard to understand, but they are real and must be recognized. Listening to one another and seeking understanding is the path to recognition and reconciliation. When a wound is deep and covered with a bandage, at some point, for healing to take place, the bandage must be removed. The wound is then exposed to the air. It may hurt, and be uncomfortable, but is necessary for healing to take place. So it is with the wounds of racial hurt and division. We must take the bandage off; expose the issues to the air so God can bring healing.

Recognition comes in the realizing that all too often the church has been complacent in causing division rather than healing. Like a church sitting above a slave dungeon, in a slave castle, where untold horrors were happening, with a Bible verse engraved above the door that says, "Here is the resting place of God . . . ." It comes in realizing that without God there can be no healing. It is he who gives us the ministry of reconciliation. It happens when we love the Lord God with all of our heart, mind, and strength, and love our neighbor as ourselves. Recognition comes when we realize that we are of one human family and are, by far, more similar than different. It happens when we can hear God say to all he has made, "that's good." In the eyes of God our Creator, every race, color, gender, person, is good. By God's grace, we can be good to each other. When the world sees the church as one, setting the example, then the world can know there is hope and that it can be done. If only we believe and make love our priority.

1. See Alexander, *The New Jim Crow*.

Part II

Imagine that you are a part of a vibrant, flourishing community located in the heart of a bustling urban epicenter. Do you first take notice of the landscape and ornate architecture or the style and class of the community and its people? Do you notice the posh boutiques and fresh markets amidst doctors and law offices, pharmacies, banks, and bakeries? Or the grand theaters, lively music venues, and the myriad of other successful businesses? As you walk the lively streets you are enthralled with the melodious harmony of unity rather than discord as many different worlds collide and a sense of pride and belonging overtake you because you realize you are a part of something spectacular, something bigger than you.

What would you think if I told you this community actually existed at the turn of the century in a post-slavery enclave? What I described in vivid detail is what *Fortune* magazine called, "the richest Negro street in the world," in 1956, a neighborhood of extreme black influence. Yes, even in the deep south steeped in a tradition of racial hate, white pride, and prejudice there was a burgeoning of a different kind of culture; a growing phenomenon in Atlanta, Georgia called "the black middle class." Auburn Avenue existed as the nucleus of the neighborhood called Sweet Auburn, coined by John Wesley Dobbs. Dobbs, an African American civic and political leader, was known as its unofficial "mayor." He, like many black Atlantans of the day, would become an integral part of the fabric of Sweet Auburn, giving it its newfound national status. Along with it, five historically black academic institutions (Morehouse College for men, Spellman College for women, Atlanta University, Clark College, and Morris Brown) would radically redefine and reshape our perspective of black people and the communities they lived in during this era. As a constructed black utopia of sorts, rich with well-trained civic, academic, and religious leaders, it was naturally the fertile training ground for some of the world's greats, including Rev. Dr. Martin Luther King, Jr., who had his beginnings right on Auburn Avenue.

Even in the wake of the racist Jim Crow era, the pride, resilience, and fortitude of the African American people in Atlanta gave hope to King that "we shall overcome." He would later go on to highlight these three aforementioned formidable forces (pride, resilience, and fortitude) in his ideology of the "beloved community." In the beloved community, poverty, hunger, and homelessness will not be tolerated because international standards of human decency will not allow it. Racism and all forms of discrimination, bigotry, and prejudice will be replaced by an all-inclusive spirit of sisterhood and brotherhood. The beloved community would not be void of conflict, but King believed the beloved community would be a place where conflicts would be resolved peacefully and adversaries could be reconciled through mutual, determined commitment to nonviolence. Long after his untimely death we continue attempts to revive this philosophy around the world. His familial legacy, first through his late wife Coretta Scott King, and then daughter Bernice, have both made tremendous strides of their own in the ever-thriving Sweet Auburn community.

On the heels of great leaders such as these, my wife and I moved into the neighborhood of Sweet Auburn in 2013, during what was the return of urban development in Atlanta since the great economic downturns of 2005 and 2008. Coming from Thomas Jefferson's great University of Virginia, we had only on occasion tasted what our millennial generation and Gen X peers called "the ATL" or the "Black Mecca"; where educated African Americans, young and old alike, could live, work, and play, enjoying the same careers, lifestyle, and luxuries often still reserved in small college towns for our white "majority culture" counterparts. Leaving the historically white institution of UVA for Atlanta with our American dream in hand seemed to be eerily reminiscent of our predecessors leaving the South for the hope of the great North during the 1960s. Yet once in Atlanta, it was at the prophetic call of our ultra hipster and majority culture pastor that we abandoned the dream of the gated enclave of black exclusivity to pick up the tattered pieces of Dr. King's beloved community. Once a beacon of hope to blacks all over the world, now Sweet Auburn barely resembled its former self and struggled to stand amidst a well-manicured national park in MLK's honor. Stakeholder institutions of faith like Ebenezer, Big Bethel, Wheat Street Baptist, and Our Lady of Lordes stand within attempts to revive the beloved community.

The dream of a reconciled community seems to be buried under classism, a grand attempt to remove every class that doesn't fit into this well thought out, grandiose plan of the new urban place—an all-inclusive, yet intentionally predetermined class, the "new urbanite." At first glance, there is no longer a need to dialogue about the issue of race in this new urban setting. Somehow we have started to believe that moving into these predetermined spaces where our God-given differences can be minimized to shared spaces such as restaurants and shopping centers solves the world's (or at the very least Atlanta's) race issue. "Careful," shouts our conscience;

could we be on the verge of yet again igniting the destructive flames of Jim Crow's reconstruction of the South?

I see majority culture millennials and Gen Xers moving into newly constructed, repurposed, renovated homes and industrial buildings alongside those owned by minorities. And yet, they can both be seen running/walking the coveted Atlanta Beltline through the once "dark town" into the historic Piedmont Park, the place of Booker T. Washington's controversial speech, "The Great Compromise." "Surely you aren't claiming race to still be an issue in Atlanta," says my black hipster friend, a second-year history major at Georgia State as we converse about the vintage feel of the Arden's Garden she's serving me in. This same student would later admit knowing nothing about Sweet Auburn's rich history, the Atlanta Life Building across the street, nor that her workplace was the original building of Atlanta's first and still running African American newspaper (even though the original sign and historic preservation plaque still hangs just outside the door).

Suddenly my well-educated wife and I realized, like this young lady, we've ascribed to a new kind of beloved community, one in which many are oftentimes excluded and removed because of class, socioeconomic status, and posh exclusive practices. Is the urban epicenter of Atlanta becoming like those exclusive all-black gated communities of the southern suburbs; replicas of their identical twin, the all-exclusive white gated communities of the northern suburbs? Are we opting out of the necessary conflict, so eloquently described in the beloved community philosophy, for a better and easier class-based community? These have become the basis of foundational dialogue and thought processes as we intentionally strive daily to live out the ideals of Dr. King's philosophy. For my wife and I, this is rooted in our ever-evolving relationship with history, people, and institutions, starting with those still alive in the Sweet Auburn community today. These people are a part of the fabric of a historic landmark district still striving to preserve and restore itself in the wake of amazing innovation and development, all while struggling to address the systemic issues of/related to poverty such as crime and homelessness. Contending as believers with the hard truth of a still segregated, racially biased, Bible Belt church of the South and their descendants (many of who admittedly are now unbelievers with no desire to be connected to the church), yet both working to diligently oppose one another and simultaneously meet the needs of the least and majority of these.

Our goal is to radically shift personal and external perspectives by continually immersing ourselves into conflicting contexts. As such, we attend and serve as college leaders at a well-known majority culture church doing so through relationships and intentionally building bridges back to my own culture. In addition, we built a house in this historically affluent black neighborhood hoping to shift the tide and influx of majority culture. Finally this calling has caused me to change the trajectory of my career from collegiate ministry to urban community development, focusing specifically on the Sweet Auburn community. This means that in my personal life, career, and ministry I commit to the ideals of restoring this beloved community by entering willingly and peaceably into the conflict of all kinds in order to achieve once again the reality of the beloved community as the cultural norm.

Bibliography

Alexander, Michelle. *The New Jim Crow: Mass Incarceration in the Age of Colorblindness.* New York: The New Press, 2012.

Du Bois, W. E. B. *The Souls of Black Folk.* New York: Millennium, 2014.

— Chapter 7 —

Art and the Art of Reconciliation

William Massey

The process of artistic creation is an incredibly effective way to witness the joining of lives. Art turns cold people warm, offers oppressed people liberation, puts anxious people at ease, helps older people feel young, and esteems forgotten people with value. Pragmatically speaking, from the outside looking in, the physical act of making art appears unnecessary. But it is an unequivocal, unexplainable catalyst for connection (both internal and external) when you are willing to give it a shot under the wing of humility. I have witnessed creative interaction bridge enormous societal gaps and build community while individually empowering the poorest in spirit. Art is one powerfully effective way to deconstruct the barriers that separate people from not only each other, but also the true self.

Before art broke down my own walls, my personality overflowed with angst. From a young age I was easily irritated, angered, and volatile. On most occasions when my parents asked me to tell them how I was feeling, to tell the truth, or to be honest, nine times out of ten I would immediately break down into tears or become enraged. I just didn't know how to articulate what was going on inside me. I was constantly frustrated and overly concerned with how others perceived me. Endless thoughts consumed my mind—anxiety, doubt, fear, confusion regarding how to manage my inner reality—and it irritated the hell out of me that I couldn't figure it out or even begin to express myself.

Ten years on and nothing much had changed other than my increasing ability to conceal the angst inside. As a young adult fresh out of high school heading thoughtlessly to college like all my peers, the pursuit of success by the world's standards trumped all else. Money, status, and self-indulgence were my main drivers. I pursued them with sporadic and temporary satisfaction, but with an underlying foundation of misery and purposelessness. The longer I pursued those things I "should" pursue, the more I realized their perpetual emptiness. I was miserable as I became increasingly aware of how tagging along after society's standards was increasingly detrimental to my soul.

Two years into business and communications classes I recognized that the most enjoyment I found in college was doodling in the columns of my notes and drawing designs on my favorite hat. Once I finally admitted to myself that I found no purpose or satisfaction within the search for wealth and job security, I decided to focus on what brought me joy. On a gut-faith impulse, I switched my major to art and immediately found purpose and passion and zeal. I finally cared about investing in something. Though art was totally illogical by society's standards, creativity spoke deeper to me than any worldly pursuit ever had.

As I immersed myself in studying and creating art I slowly discovered how to release the ambiguous inner workings within myself—the part of me unable to encapsulate in language, yet truest to who I really am. I see now that partaking in the act of creating was a step towards acknowledging my Creator. Like God, art isn't nearly as powerful if you don't get your hands dirty through investigating, practicing, and deepening relationship. It is an indescribable, intangible feeling one must dive straight into in order to understand, like feeling weightless in a body of water. Once you partake in the process of creation, the instant you make something out of nothing, you feel the activation inside yourself which is closer to the peace and power of the Creator than we typically experience in our basic, worldly survival routine.

Diving into an art degree I knew I was closer to my purpose, but while I was creating in the studio for hours upon hours I continued to feel a disconnect. I had found my passion, but was not satisfied working alone, making art for me, then nailing it to a gallery wall for others after the fact. Despite generally liking what I was pursuing, there was still a longing in me, this innate need to directly interact with and impact others for good through my passion. I began to consider that since I had found art to be the key to unlock what was once stuck inside my soul, maybe I could help others carve out their key too.

One Friday afternoon I was headed toward the liquor store after class. As I passed by the hospital something inside me turned my car into the parking lot. I walked into the building with no plan and no agenda. I had no idea of what I was doing there, but I ended up at volunteer services. I said something like, "Could I . . . just maybe . . . like . . . make art with people who aren't having a very good day?" They sent me to the cancer center.

The first patient I ever sat next to in the cancer center was William, an older Vietnam veteran. It began as a clunky and awkward interaction. I didn't know what to say and couldn't think of what to do so I pulled out a pad of paper and drew as William answered my question about what he ate for breakfast. The awkwardness broke after a couple minutes as we both looked down and saw how ridiculous the drawing of his egg burrito was. We laughed.

I had no idea what I was doing making art with patients at that hospital in south Georgia. I just felt like I needed to be there. I was petrified yet continued to keep showing up week after week, encouraging others to get out of their heads and help pass the time by goofing off creatively. Though it was consistently fruitful, not a volunteer day passed where the purveyor of resistance didn't try to talk me out of going to the cancer center. Every morning was a different excuse, but I continuously fought to sit down with those people facing mortality to make art with them. All I knew was the second I arrived, sat next to the patient, and introduced myself, all doubt fled. As soon as the person in front of me realized I had no agenda besides passing time creatively and loving them well, the atmosphere changed. The patients transitioned from dwelling on fear, mortality, and uncertainty . . . to a feeling of relation, control, and enjoyment. They were redirected from obsessing over their condition to exploring a light-hearted, positive shift in focus.

I learned at the hospital that art is metamorphic. Sometimes it's simply an entrance to relaxed, therapeutic, and vulnerable conversation. In other instances, conversation eases an individual into creative release that heals and breaks up inner turmoil that no amount of talking ever could.

Following graduation and some nomadic world travel, I eventually moved to Atlanta to figure out what a career in art looked like. I allowed resistance to keep me from my calling for about a year before I began walking with a bag of art supplies into places of distress again. First a health and hospice home, then another cancer center, a homeless community, and so on. I gently eased people into making art, and the more who gave it a try, the more they would realize the power it held—it was infectious in the most life-giving way. I began rediscovering art as not only a personal reconciler, but a community cultivator as well. Individuals within the same facility, hardened and separated, began to come alive and be unified through trying something new, creative, and intriguing together. Taking leaps together. Being vulnerable together.

During this time, "intuition" again took the reins—I had no plan other than simply making art with people and establishing light-hearted yet profound bridges of connection. Looking back now I realize I was toning my muscles of social and empathetic discernment—learning how to best connect with and encourage each unique person I encountered. You can tell a lot about a person by how they scribble on a piece of paper—and they'll tell you a lot about themselves while doing so. I became acutely aware of who was in front of me, not what they presented, but what I sensed underneath the initial appearance. In essence I was growing my ability to be present. Eventually I began helping to spark youthful life in isolated older adults who had been generally unresponsive. Chronically homeless men would transition from removed and fear-based to engaging and love-based in their interactions. Cancer patients in the most difficult period of their battle were smiling again and cracking jokes. Provoking those happenings was the highest high I'd ever felt. But inevitably, after every incredible stimulus of invigorating human connection—no matter how beautiful the artwork or interaction—the deep, unquenchable longing remained in me. I was as close as I'd ever been to "it," yet I knew I still didn't have "it."

At this point, doing all the "right" things but still feeling an imposing emptiness, I turned to Jesus. I had honestly put my trust and time into everything else I could possibly think of and was left wanting. There were bursts of fulfillment, but no sustaining joy—no eternal peace. After self-indulgence, substances, sex, education, world travel, a successful early career in sculpture, endless altruism, a "healthy" romantic relationship, meditation, exercise, reading, eating right, a growing family, an obedient dog . . . I finally realized the things of this world could never satisfy my thirst. Furthermore I hadn't found any way to frame the illogical calling in my heart to serve others through the act of creation. Entertaining the idea of Jesus was my last resort. So I grew some humility and sought the man who claimed to be the Way, the Truth, and the Life. And truly, if I had not sifted through everything else before arriving at Christ, I wouldn't have encountered him the way I did.

Before developing a relationship with Jesus, I had no idea why I was drawn towards creatively engaging people in difficult situations. Now it's through the lens of Jesus that I finally understand these gravitations in my heart. First, we are called by God to die to our own desires and serve our neighbors. Second, we are called by God to be co-creators on this earth; our vocation as human beings is literally to bring divine creation forth. I see clearly now that God was using my talents and mysterious desires to pull me closer to a relationship with Christ all along. I said yes to creation, yes to the broken, and Christ-in-me utilized my partial willingness for his good until I finally submitted everything else I had to him. I never felt complete until I felt Jesus inside my heart. Again, this most powerful experience will never be fully encapsulated in words—I felt it and I knew it.

Nothing much changed in my practices after beginning to trust Christ in lieu of myself. I did the same stuff with the same materials with the same people. The only thing that changed was my sustained security and peace despite the reactions of others; a kind of assurance in myself and my calling. Before I knew Jesus, my self-worth was determined by how good I did. The motives of my work were well-disguised yet completely self-centered—using art to make others feel better so that at the end of the day I felt good, successful, and happy. What changed is that I now love others by first *receiving* that peace through Christ, as opposed to manifesting that peace through my own work. My burden of insufficiency has been removed. True Life and true fulfillment no longer comes from my doing, it's an inside job of accepting what has already been done, and what I will never obtain through my own strength.

One of the best parts of God revelation is the more I give up my own motives and humble myself to play a part in his, the effectiveness of creativity sparking breakthrough exponentially increases. The only thing I need is a childlike faith to trust God's eternal plan above my own temporal perspective. Now I'm simply a kid trusting Dad's lead, even when I don't feel like it—especially when I don't feel like it.

Imagine this: two adults on either side of a table, you tell them, "connect, be friends." What happens? Immediate pressure, false identities, interaction halted by layers of societal conversation protocol, and lack of organic flow.

Imagine this: You put a piece of paper in front of two people and tell them to scribble. What happens? The child in them comes out. The same awkward, goofy child that makes friends easily and isn't stifled by rules and boundaries. Art transforms us to have a childlike openness. Without thinking too hard or forcing it, we are inclined to be less critical and more congenial with one another when we create for the sake of creating. And slowly we grow out of the habit to be critical and beat ourselves up. Art provides a path to be carefree kids again—which I believe is the red-hot center of God's heart for us.

Whenever I put art supplies in front of somebody, especially if they haven't created since they were a kid, I make sure they understand there is no expectation for perfection or a masterpiece, there is no right or wrong. Just do you. As long as we are willing to give art a try and leave behind the thoughts of "I'm not an artist, I'm not creative, I'm no good," there is either an instant shattering or a gradual dissolving of the crusty baggage that the world has smeared over who we really are. The power of creation is universal; beyond language, status, and social class. It levels the playing field. And no matter where art is created, joy and connection are inevitable.

It's funny that most people I talk to say, "I haven't made art since I was a kid." Why is it that the most carefree, playful, often mentally wholesome time in our lives is the same period in which we create art most? Is there something connecting the joy-filled aspect of our childhood, letting down our guard, not thinking too much, and goofing off with making art? Are we really supposed to lose that sense of freedom and creativity when we grow older? Are our minds meant to shift to think that it is unnecessary? Are we really meant to subdue more and create less? No. We are destined to be co-creators with God. Greater works will we do.

REMERGE builds intentional communities of diverse persons with the intent of fostering reconciliation. Many members of the central Atlanta community are from the chronically homeless population. When I first started coming to REMERGE I met one of the more charismatic community members—his name is Rico. Rico lives on the streets, has the reputation of a pipe bomb, and has eyes that can bend steel. Rico used to be unapproachable, hardened, and honestly straight-up scary. Even by the REMERGE community he was well-integrated into, he was feared and revered based on a lengthy history of volatile and violent outbreaks. Rico was nearly impossible to communicate with for more than a moment. He wouldn't mingle, interact, and especially wouldn't sit within twenty feet of the art activities. But the more I kept showing up and putting out the art supplies, the more he saw how relaxed, low-key, and noninvasive the process of making art can be. Rico was softened slowly, week after week, month after month, as he observed others willingly and happily participating. After six months, he sat at the same table as the art supplies. A month later, he picked up a pencil and made a mark.

Now, each day I show up to do art with the community Rico has typically already started to create. He is a fiend! Chatting and laughing, smiling and teasing while he doodles. I have regularly seen him forgetting about lunch to leave his mark on whatever project is in front of him. From a life of living on streets, constantly worried about losing what little you have left, Rico had come to learn that art is life-giving, not taking. These days, when I see Rico, he embraces me with a hug and a smile. I believe art helped to heal him, or at least softened his heart for a relationship to do so.

A lot of people make art *about* activism or make art *about* God. But what I find far more meaningful is sparking experiences where creating *is* activism, where God is found in the process, not the product.

I must say though, despite all the challenges of provoking people to make art, the most difficult aspects of creatively joining lives have nothing to do with engaging people—it's the time before and after the interactions. It's getting up in the morning and feeling like I'd rather not go into a room of people fighting for survival. It's finishing a workshop and driving back to my house, leaving my friend to walk away down the street he calls home. It's departing the cancer center to meet up with friends at the park while the patients go home to feel excruciatingly miserable for two weeks until their next chemotherapy treatment. The most difficult part of joining lives is the enemy that works so tirelessly to get me to believe the path I'm on isn't doing a damn thing.

A friend of mine once told me about her experience facilitating an art project with the children of an orphanage in rural Tanzania. She began the first day by holding a fly-covered baby with a stomach swollen from malnutrition, while pouring paint out for the other children and informing them to not eat the color. Immediately my friend was consumed with guilt, regarding both the validity of making art at the orphanage as well as feeling like a naïve, rich white girl who oversimplifies charity and the needs of the poor. Later that evening she was preparing materials for the next day, all the while consumed with conflicted feelings of her ability to execute her motives in a thoughtful and dignifying way. At that moment an older humanitarian researcher passed through the common area on his way to the next assignment and shared a smile over the rare encounter of another *muzungu* (white person). She immediately fired the question at him of whether what she was doing holds any value in light of his research. The humanitarian responded with wisdom acquired through years of interacting with and interviewing refugees, displaced and tormented persons. He explained to her that most groups attempting to perform "charity" just treat people like dogs—supplying food, water, and shelter without regard for what lies beyond basic needs. The man shared that the most astounding atrocities he'd ever researched or witnessed weren't based on stripping people of basic needs, but rather robbing them of their dignity. He went deeper, describing interviews where people would casually speak of torture and horrendous conditions, but describe in-depth the time someone stopped to teach them how to whittle a stick, sing a song, or paint a painting. The most impactful memories weren't based on survival as much as those rare moments that added value and enjoyment *to* survival. People felt most honored, most alive, when they had the liberty to freely create for nothing more than the joy of creation.

Dumping goods and services on people without joining lives is an easy, wide door to walk through. You can give someone a meal, a coat, or a buck with a flick of the wrist . . . but unequivocal impact is made through intentional, vulnerable, raw relationship. That's what Jesus is all about. He is calling us to co-create with him, take some leaps, connect with some souls, let down our guard, be a kid again, and leave your (and his) mark.

— Chapter 8 —

Disability and Reconciliation
The Old Woman's Model

Stephanie Brock and Brian Brock

A woman in Vancouver recently caused an Internet sensation by recounting a remarkable encounter she witnessed. Travelling in a public train carriage, Ehab Taha found herself near a man acting aggressively and erratically. To everyone's great surprise an older woman seated near him took his hand and held on to it, a gesture that within minutes had calmed him and eventually brought tears to his eyes. Puzzled by this unexpected outcome, which she also captured in a memorable picture, Ehab comments: "I spoke to the woman after this incident and she simply said, 'I'm a mother and he needed someone to touch.'" Then the older woman herself began to weep.[1]

In such stories we begin to glimpse the need for and also the mechanics of a ministry of reconciliation in its relation to disability. The angry and erratic man displays for us the anguish that a person can suffer as they absorb their utter aloneness in a crowd of people whom they utterly terrify. What can be done for this man? Who can deal with him, who can subdue him and keep innocent bystanders safe from his travails? Where one might

1. Hot Topics, "Woman on train holds man's hand when everyone else is too scared to approach him."

say "social services" and another "the police," this woman, one of the more frail members of society if her photograph on Facebook is to be taken at face value, says simply: "it is me, he calls to me for help." She knows from her experience being a mother what he needs. He needs love. He needs to know that another human being values him enough to listen and connect with him. It is a story, we will see, that comes in countless variations in the world of mental disability, in that it touches on all the situations of life encountered by those whose minds are unruly, seem to be fading, or who have never possessed the ability to communicate well.

But while this story is a beautiful example of the impact of a ministry of reconciliation, it offers no textbook answer about how to follow this example. A hand held would not calm every person in every situation. This suggests that it is not what happened, where, or to whom that matters here: *it is that one person can be moved in their core to surmount obvious social barriers to connect with another person on an emotional and human level.* Our suggestion in this chapter will be that talk about the issue of disability and reconciliation most fruitfully begins by asking what we can learn from the "old woman."

Examining the Links between Mental Health and Social Vulnerability

We all begin life in the same way: adjusting to and learning to survive in a blindingly different environment from the one in which we had previously been nurtured. And in our new and frightening environment we discover that we need to be cared for and loved. We are completely vulnerable, and rely on the others around us to meet our every need, physical and emotional. Another part of our adjustment as human beings is to begin to express basic needs and to communicate—in very rudimentary ways at first which progress over time as development progresses. As babies we ask by crying alone: as time goes on that "asking" takes further shape. Thus at its most basic level, human life begins with two basic needs: the need to be loved and the need to communicate oneself to others.

Though fragile and imperfect in the best of scenarios, many people find a way to meet these needs to some degree at least some of the time. However, in a world where mental health disorders have risen to the level of tens of millions affected, and only half of those receive treatment, we are bound to encounter a breakdown of this exchange process at some point.

The National Institute of Mental Health estimates that "neuropsychiatric disorders are the leading cause of disability in the U.S." and that the majority of these disorders are of a mental and/or behavioral origin.[2] In fact, mental and behavioral disorder is the leading category of disease for people up to the age of about seventy-five. This means that of all the things that might cause injury, burden, or quality of life loss for a person of any age below seventy-five, the likelihood statistically is that it will be a mental health disorder.

Breaking this statistic down further, over the course of their lifetime roughly 20 percent of adults will have some form or degree of mental illness. That means that roughly one in five adults walking around will be experiencing some degree of a breakdown in their mental, intellectual or emotional processes. And this of course isn't just on American soil. The WHO reported in 2002 that 450 million people worldwide suffer from some form of mental health illness, with depression and drug and alcohol addiction topping the charts as contributing factors, and incarceration also being closely linked with mental illness.[3]

Mental health and illness can be seen on a continuum, and as such is part of the wider category of disability. With regard to the statistics on disability, we find that, depending on the study, roughly 12–19 percent of Americans live with some form of disability.[4] That's around 56.7 million people.[5] Only about 34 percent of people with a disability between the ages of twenty-one and sixty-four are employed. And the most worrying statistic of all is that of these millions of men, women, and children with a disability, roughly 28 percent live at or below the poverty line.

These kinds of statistics reveal an epidemic. Where disability and mental illness are present we see an associated breakdown in one's ability to express their need for love and closeness and communicate themselves to others. This breakdown ultimately impacts their family, their wider relationships, and their ability to function in community, and often results in alienation, poverty, further illness, and burden on society. And this breakdown is on the rise globally. Evidence suggests that mental illness is rife

2. Murray et al., "The state of US health, 1990–2010," 591–608.

3. World Health Organization, "Investing in Mental Health."

4. See http://disabilitystatistics.org.

5. U.S. Census Bureau. http://www.disabled-world.com/disability/statistics/info.php.

among the homeless population.[6] All this indicates primarily that any approach to the plight of the social outcast that overlooks the issue of mental health will quickly be undermined.

It is important to acknowledge the differences between congenital conditions that affect mental functioning, such as Down's syndrome, and mental illnesses like bipolar disorder. Both may be alleviated by thoughtful treatment regimes, though the likelihood of complete restoration of what we think of as normal mental and emotional functioning is highly unlikely in most of these cases. The reason for this is that the human mind is not something that can easily be "fixed" since it is so interweaved with how we perceives ourselves and how others perceive us.

This is not to suggest that all conditions that appear to compromise people's powers of cognitive or emotional processing are equal. Some conditions like bipolar disorder, or some forms of autism or hyper reactivity may engender more threatening or aggressive behaviors, behaviors which can easily end in homelessness when the patience of friends and caring institutions runs out. Some of these conditions can also be catalyzed by drug use, which inevitably leads to the moral stigmatization of those who end up homeless, addicted, and mentally ill as "deserving it." We must come to terms with the reality that in the modern West we often think of the average person with Down's syndrome as morally innocent and largely non-threatening and likable, while the shabbily dressed homeless person who talks to themselves appears to us as tragic, threatening, and as likely having brought their condition on themselves. These are the commonsense prejudices that drive us away from those who live the pain of human estrangement in especially acute ways, both the pains that drove their self-destructive behaviors and the pains that have resulted from their coping strategies.

Extensive empirical research has been done on the effects of mental illness on individuals and communities given the extensive impact of such conditions on individuals, family systems, caregivers, and communities.[7] What emerges is a clear picture of the many ways in which an individual with a mental health illness or disability is often quite vulnerable, prone to poverty, and isolated through mobility issues or social exclusion that can very easily lead them into conditions of homelessness. Families and caregivers can suffer exhaustion and concurrent isolation as they care

6. Mercier and Picard, "Intellectual disability and homelessness," 441–49.

7. Department of Mental Health and Substance Dependence, Noncommunicable Diseases and Mental Health, World Health Organization, "Investing in Mental Health."

for their loved one, along with depression, physical and emotional problems, financial strain, and the lack of their own life and individuality. And communities may find their resources strained to provide adequate health care, lost revenue from unemployment or sick leave, increasing violence, dangerous behaviors such as drug and alcohol misuse and incarceration rates, among other dynamics.

The purpose of this chapter, however, is not to understand the etiology of such a phenomenon but instead to look at what might be done to alleviate some of its most destructive impacts. In short, if mental illness and disability are all around us, and they are having an often negative and destructive impact on peoples' lives and the communities in which we live, what can we do about it? Christians know that the story we read in the papers or the journal articles documenting doom and destruction is not the only story we have been given. We have been told a story about a God who comes into the world to change it, to love it, and redeem it to himself. How then can and should we reconcile ourselves to this world for which our Savior gave his life? How can and should we be actors for reconciliation between the world that suffers mental, physical, and emotional anguish and the Creator who longs for wholeness for his creation?

Vulnerability as Invitation

The first clear directive given to each of us is to act in accordance with what we have been given. Going back to the opening story, the elderly woman on the train had no information about the agitated man. She had no diagnosis, no life history, and certainly had no assurance that her action would be well-received. Her intervention was not "well-informed." Nevertheless, she forged ahead by simply reaching out, and in so doing she modeled an exemplary refusal to live constricted by her fears in a situation involving behavior outside what we would conceive of as our normal comfort zone.

To make oneself vulnerable in this way is to move into the working space of the Holy Spirit. We can call acts undertaken in this space part of the "mystery of compassion." Compassion is a particularly interesting word, given the time of its origin. It is a combination of the Latin roots "*com*" and "*passio*," "*com*" meaning "with" and "*passio*" meaning "suffering." Arising around AD 6 in the thoroughly Christianized Middle Ages, the term was coined to link the suffering of every human being with the passion of Christ. Because Christians confess that Christ suffered for us and our sins, we confess having known his desire to be present to every human being in their sin and brokenness. To respond with compassion is then, theologically understood, essentially to respond to *God's* love for another suffering human being.

This is why we must speak of action toward the vulnerable, by Christians whose *own* vulnerability has and is being revealed, as the work of an intermediary. People who are hurting and confused need to be coaxed out into a relationship of trust by someone who respects them, does not wish to manipulate them or impose something on them. Before solutions and fixes are proposed, however good they might be, Jean Vanier suggests, "the intermediary must first discover the beauty of the wounded person, hidden under the fears, the depression and the violence. In effect, to love is not primarily *to do* something for someone, but it is *to reveal* to that person his or her value, not only through listening and tenderness, through love and kindness, but also through a certain competence and faithful commitment."[8]

To receive the gift of compassion as capable of moving beyond fear requires an active decision on our part, often a very disciplined and intense decision to act in ways we do not find comfortable. Such acts are not only counterintuitive but countercultural in resisting the ways that society has taught us to act. But as we do so we move into a space where persons are not reduced to their behavior or appearance. Instead, their creaturely being in its goodness is apprehended as the light of their redemption falls on them from the work of Jesus. It is in this space beyond fear that true reconciliation is born, for that is where a person is most hurting, most lonely, and most in need of the love of another human being. In this space we might just be able to hold out a hand and by doing so dissipate the fear of another person, if only for a moment. It is this overcoming of our fears of the other, fears born in the estrangement of our capacity to communicate with one another at Babel, that is the central work of the Holy Spirit (Acts 2; 1 Cor 12).

Secondly, as an actor for reconciliation we connect our experience with that of another human being. We all know pain and sorrow, we all know joys and disappointments. We all know sickness and despair as well as we know health and stability. Some people in our midst are simply going to know more despair and more illness than others, but that does not mean they enter into another category of human that is different from us. They

8. Vanier, *Man and Woman God Made Them*, 18.

never become "those people" for we are all on the same continuum: I in my health and relative stability of life and relationships, and you in your drug addiction that has led to homelessness and poverty, isolation and mental illness. We are not different in kind, because my sin and addictions may not have been so visibly ramified, but they remain just as ugly and destructive in the eyes of a loving God who wishes that we be made whole.

The old woman on the train saw this when she looked at the agitated man. She saw herself as a mother caring for her children, she saw him as a child needing a mother's touch. She saw that his need equaled what she would need in the same situation because he is as human as she is, with the same needs and desires. When she reached out to him it was as someone who has acknowledged in herself the humanity in the person before her. As a mother she remembered that when a baby cries you comfort it, you hold it—you give it love and meet its needs. In the people all around us, where is the need that might be met by us in this moment?

Jean Vanier has thought deeply about the way that we internalize the rejections we have experienced in our human relationships. When a child reaches out to be loved, if it meets violence and coldness, defenses are built up, scars will accrue. This is true of all human beings, and is part of what we mean when we talk about sin. Children and adults who have learned that they are not loved find it hard to believe themselves to be lovable. They find it equally hard to give to others what they haven't learned to receive themselves. This logic is relentless. This is why physical connection and even the way we look at others touches on and can confront people's self-image. Jean Vanier summarizes the crucial issue at stake:

> There is always a message transmitted with our eyes: it can be approval, affection, indifference, scorn, distaste, etc. When we constantly avoid looking at certain persons, they immediately sense rejection or repulsion. Over time they will have the feeling of being worthless, even to themselves. Eventually, they too will avoid looking at themselves. This is often the story for those excluded from our society because of a disability or other reasons.[9]

The gesture of compassion of the old woman works because she confronts the self-image of a man who believes he is not loved, is angry, and wishes to inflict his suffering on those around him. It is not easy to resist reinforcing the rejection of the masses, which is why we need the working of the God of love in us to venture such a risky embrace.

9. Ibid., 9–10.

Finally, the true core of any ministry of reconciliation with our broken and dark world is the impact that it has on our own person when we connect with it. The old woman cried after she came off the train. We might wonder why she cried when asked to explain why she took the young man's hand. And the reason is because his humanity touched her. She felt deep in her heart both the need this man had that he simply could not reasonably express to anyone else at that moment, and the part of her that had been forever changed by their encounter.

Responding Vulnerably to the Call of the Vulnerable

People who suffer from conditions such as disability and mental illness are ultimately vulnerable, and they expose our vulnerability. If their response to their own sense of vulnerability is erratic or aggressive the most common response to the sense of social vulnerability amongst polite and literate society is a distanced coolness and quick evasiveness. Try to imagine what it must be like to know that you are constantly looked down upon by society as "abnormal" and suspected to be lazy or a potential thief. Consider what it would be like to have no idea why you never have satisfactory interactions with other people around you, not being able to communicate your basic needs (you might not even know what they are), and sensing that you are never truly loved. Or perhaps you don't even know what it means to be truly loved. You might have even been told that Jesus can offer this kind of love, but you certainly have never felt his hand through another person.

The darkness of that lived experience will make people act in ways that society deems irresponsible, or dangerous, or simply unsightly. They are ultimately explainable, but we often lose sight of that fact. And it is in the realization of the darkness that another person might live in that our hearts are pierced just as Jesus' heart was pierced when he wept for those around him. We cannot help but weep too when we have encountered someone else in the dark place that Christ came to banish. And as ministers of reconciliation, we are called to witness to Christ's reconciling work. Not just by telling people "about" it, but by the "body preaching" that shows what the message of Jesus Christ means in the touch and love that reaches out across the abyss to try and connect with the person who lives in such darkness. But for Christ's love and his calling out to me and bringing me home, there too would I be living.

Christ calls us as his ministers to be unafraid to accompany him as he goes with humanity into its darkest and messiest corners. He calls us to be present to those in need, in a real way and with as much real physical presence as we can manage. This is at the same time to call us to acknowledge our own vulnerability by engaging with our own humanity, its repulsions and needs, as we respond to this call.

This engagement is always ours alone, but it is never all on our own. Hans Reinders has explained in some detail why modern social welfare systems can never provide what the mentally ill and disabled most desperately need: friends. Social welfare nets can provide for some of the material and even some of the social needs of the vulnerable, but they can never mandate the enduring engagement that makes up friendship. Christians are for extending the rights of the social outcast (such as to health care) and to refusing their exclusion from public space (such as by resisting the criminalization of panhandling or sleeping rough), but these presumptions for some social policies over others, Reinders insists, can never replace the basic stuff of human love.

> Rights open doors, not hearts. Hearts must be opened in order
> for people to know how to be present with human beings who
> don't speak, who are restless, who may be imprisoned by destruc-
> tive impulses, who do not have the ability to fix their attention, or
> who even don't have a sense of who they are or what they want
> for themselves. In spite of all these varying characteristics, they
> nonetheless all share in the human need to be loved. Being loved
> is being needed, and being needed is more than existing merely as
> a bunch of problems to be solved.[10]

If Christians are committed to this vulnerable love then institutions will inevitably spring up that serve and foster it, inviting more people in. We can understand lives like that of Jean Vanier as exemplary for Christians in the obvious vulnerability of his living with the outcasts of his society. This example has been so luminous that it has spawned a global movement called L'Arche. Because the church is trapped in a world that values power and success, the young of the modern, western-developed world are hungry for touch, friendship, and connection, like everyone else in modern society. They must be led, he suggests, "to *true* community where they can become men and women of prayer and compassion, open to others and to the world, particularly to the poor, the oppressed, the lost, and the

---

10. Reinders, *Receiving the Gift of Friendship*, 187.

vulnerable, and thus become 'artisans of peace.'"[11] The old woman with whom we began was one such artisan of peace, who displayed the power of skills learned in community with the vulnerable, children, and so called all who saw her to a new way of life.

This movement, Stanley Hauerwas has often noted, would make no sense if the gospel of Jesus Christ is not true.[12] In communities like L'Arche, as in countless other intentional Christian communities, we see what it concretely means that Christians have discovered a Jesus Christ who has not come to "do something for us" but, because he loves us, to be with us. The love of Jesus Christ is not a general atmosphere but personal touch, which is why Christians call the person of this love the Holy Spirit. In this Spirit the vulnerability of the crucified Lord comes alive in concrete community through vulnerability, the call of Jesus Christ, and the obedience of discipleship. These connections are beautifully drawn together by Stanley Hauerwas and Will Willimon in the final passage from their book on the Holy Spirit. Before he leaves, Jesus tells his disciples that he is leaving them his peace, but he does so not as the world gives peace. The world tries to establish peace through half-truths, power plays, coercion, but the peace that the Holy Spirit enacts is not the bogus order secured by violence that so many call "peace." The peace of Christ comes through the work of the Holy Spirit, whose task of always pointing us to Jesus makes possible a disavowal of violence and in such a disavowal the birth of friendship.

> A pastor was appointed to an all-white church and to an all-black church located barely a mile from one another. The bishop told him that it was his task to try to bring the two congregations together.
>
> 'I was terrified. I knew that to attempt something this holy, this demanding, I would fail without the constant, miraculous intervention of the Holy Spirit.' Every morning and evening the pastor prayed earnestly for the visitation, empowerment, and guidance of the Spirit. He taught his congregations, at every turn in the road, before every decision and each new move, to pray in effect, 'Holy Spirit, if you want us to be one church, you must walk with us.'
>
> Three years later the Holy Spirit has produced one of the few truly multiracial congregations in that part of the world.[13]

11. Vanier, *Community and Growth*, 5.

12. Hauerwas, "Why Jean Vanier Matters." Also Hauerwas, "Seeing Peace."

13. Hauerwas and Willimon, *The Holy Spirit*, 82–83.

To be a reconciling community is to be a community that prays to the Lord of redemption, reconciliation, and wholeness to empower each of his children to discern the movements of his Spirit and to follow Jesus as he undertakes similarly redemptive works in our times and with our neighbors. It can be that our relatively enlightened modern western democracies mask the brokenness of the vulnerable in them. The prayer to follow Christ therefore includes a prayer to open our eyes to our own vulnerability and that of our most vulnerable neighbors, and for the boldness to respond, prayers which are summarized by the prayer of the New Testament church: "Come, Holy Spirit!"

Bibliography

Department of Mental Health and Substance Dependence, Noncommunicable Diseases and Mental Health, World Health Organization. "Investing in Mental Health." http://www.who.int/mental_health/media/investing_mnh.pdf.

Disability Statistics. http://disabilitystatistics.org.

Hauerwas, Stanley, and William H. Willimon. *The Holy Spirit*. Nashville: Abingdon, 2015.

Hauerwas, Stanley. "Why Jean Vanier Matters: An Exemplary Exploration." In *Knowing, Being Known, and the Mystery of God: Essays in Honor of Professor Hans Reinders: Teacher, Friend, Disciple*, edited by Bill Gaventa and Erik de Jongh, 229–39. Amsterdam: VU University Press, 2016.

———. "Seeing Peace: L'Arche as a Peace Movement." In *The Paradox of Disability: Responses to Jean Vanier and L'Arche Communities from Theology and the Sciences*, 113–26. Grand Rapids: Eerdmans, 2010.

Hot Topics. "Woman on train holds man's hand when everyone else is too scared to approach him." http://hottopics.tv/story/woman-on-train-holds-mans-hand-when-everyone-else-is-too-scared-to-approach-him.

Mercier, C., and S. Picard. "Intellectual disability and homelessness." *Journal of Intellectual Disability Research* 55:4 (April 2011) 441–49.

Murray, C. J., et al. "The state of US health, 1990–2010: burden of diseases, injuries, and risk factors." Journal of the American Medical Association 14:310(6) (August 2013) 591–608.

Reinders, Hans. *Receiving the Gift of Friendship: Profound Disability, Theological Anthropology, and Ethics*. Grand Rapids: Eerdmans, 2008.

US Census Bureau. http://www.disabled-world.com/disability/statistics/info.php.

Vanier, Jean. *Community and Growth*. Rev. ed. London: Darton, Longman and Todd, 1989.

———. *Man and Woman God Made Them*. London: Darton, Longman and Todd, 2007.

World Health Organization. "Investing in Mental Health." http://www.uniteforsight.org/mental-health/module1.

— Chapter 9 —

Stripped Love
Reconciliation and Sex Trafficking

Kimberly Majeski

In the opening chapters of Genesis we see the heart of God revealed. After the fall of Eden and the first murder, God calls out to Cain and inquires after Abel whom Cain has just killed. Cain's question to God's inquiry is instructive for life lived out in the ethic of God: he asks, "Am I my brother's keeper?" (Gen. 4:9). I submit that God's resounding answer across the corpus of Scripture from the call to care for the poor, the widows and orphans and aliens of the Hebrew canon, the lament of the prophets since Israel has failed to do so, Jesus' own teaching to care for the least of these, and Revelation's return to the garden, is a resounding "yes!" It is the work of every child of God, then, to love and serve and become family with the most vulnerable in her own place in the world. This is the foundation. This is the bedrock out of which my life and call and vocation is born. In my journey this biblical premise has led me to serve women in the commercial sex trade and delivered me to strip clubs across the United States of America.

In the Beginning

I had never been inside a strip club before, so I was as eager, terrified, and naïve as you can imagine. My heart on fire to do the work of God in the world, broken and compelled for women in the commercial sex trade, I had joined a friend of mine on mission to deliver warm meals to a few clubs in her town.

The music was assaulting but, oddly, the profanity ringing through the speakers felt right for such a place where all the light of the outside world had been smothered out, windows painted black, smoke so thick you could barely see your hand in front of your face. Colored lights whirled around the room at a dizzying pace and suddenly I was aware this was all a part of the transition into the realm of the sex club, where women's bodies are bought and sold with every shot of Jägermeister and turn on the VIP couch.

I was grateful to have a tub filled with plates and napkins in my hands so I was able to focus on putting one foot in front of the other and balance all the wares I was carrying. We made our way to the back of the club and the women's dressing room where we unloaded warm chicken casserole and mashed potatoes. We unwrapped the food and tidied up the place, wiping the counter and emptying ashtrays, and the dancers began to pour into the room as if the smell of a home-cooked meal had lured them into a happy trance. They were hungry, I could tell, as many of them were skin and bones, quite visible in their lace and fishnet lingerie. At once the room was filled with scantily clad women in ten-inch heels who introduced themselves as "Foxy," "Lil' Kim," "Ace," and the like. I was trying to keep up, shake hands, offer a smile as they somewhat skeptically welcomed me when the door flung open and four-letter words rang through the air. Just then a six-foot–tall blonde busted through, cursing the stage and the accident she'd just had that left her elbow gashed and spewing blood. Not to worry, my friend had first aid supplies in her trusty tub, so she quickly handed me clean gauze and Band-Aids and gestured me towards the young woman in need.

"Hi, I'm Kimberly," I said. "Can I help you clean that cut?" "Sure," she said, surveying me standing over her with supplies. "That looks bad. What happened?" I said, as if I'd seen hundreds of strip club battle wounds before. "I was spinning on the pole and cut my elbow on the f#$% ceiling tile, this piece of s#$% place," she railed. I told her I was sorry, asked her name, and she told me: "*Heaven.*" I had to pause at the irony of it. She was a towering, gorgeous woman, much younger than me, with icy blonde hair and wide green eyes the color of peridot. She was cut and bleeding, dressed only in fishnet stockings and clear plastic heels; her current situation seemed anything but heavenly.

I pressed forward to attempt to clean her cut but she took the gauze from me, preferring to do it herself. I handed her the Band-Aid. She wiped and worked as I stood over her and she would politely gaze up, smile at me, and continue her task. We talked about how cool her shoes were, how there's not really any class to teach you how to maneuver in them, and she allowed me to make her a to-go plate of chicken noodles since an important patron had arrived and was asking for her by name—Heaven.

Before I knew it, it was time to pack our things and go on to the next club. I was feeling the thrill of conquering a terrifying experience as my friend remarked on how well I had connected with the women in such a short time. She gave me only one note of direction. "Next time," she said gently, "have a seat." I couldn't believe it. She was right. I had been standing the entire time! When I saw bodies reclining on chairs, the state of that dressing room strewn with undergarments and fake hair and makeup, curling irons burning holes in the linoleum counter, something in me decided to protect myself from injury, harm, disease. Something deep inside that I was not aware of kept me standing in my designer jeans, looking down on the women whom I'd come to serve. At once I felt convicted and understood in that moment; I knew this posture would never work.

That was more than six years ago now and I have since visited hundreds of women, and served them in their place of trouble—strip clubs across the United States. Shortly after my first visit with my friend to the strip clubs in her city, we launched our own ministry to women in the commercial sex trade in central Indiana and I have shared life with some of the most incredible, resilient women I've ever known. I have been their friend and pastor and they have been my salvation. Their courage, love, and goodness has ministered to me over and over again.

As a nonprofit ministry, Stripped Love exists to empower women to walk out of fear and into love. We do this by showing up consistently and loving women as God loves them, right where they are, just as they are, and we train others to do the same. We call ourselves Stripped Love because we believe that once you strip away everything that is secondary, all that divides and separates us, all the periphery falsehood of insiders and outsiders, what is left is love, and we believe love heals.

We resolved early on that our only agenda in the clubs would be to love. There is nothing hidden about what we do or who we are; we don't ask women to walk away from their employment or leave the building singing "Onward Christian Soldiers." We just show up week after week, month after month, in rain, sleet, or snow, in good times and bad, when the coffers are full and when they're empty; we show up and we love. This is the gospel work.

It became abundantly clear to us early on that authentic friendship would be the central matter of our work. It was also apparent that it was incumbent upon us to visit our friends on their turf, to get to know their world before ever asking them to step into ours. The fact is, most of my friends from the club would never make their way to the front door of a church in the suburbs. It turns out my friends feel like the church left them behind long ago because of life choices born from harsh circumstances. Generally, my friends feel judged by the church, they feel marginalized by Christians who are supposed to be emissaries of Jesus but who don't seem to love like Jesus. What's true is that in the hard work of reconciliation the party with the perceived power has to be the one to risk enough to help the other feel safe, welcomed, wanted. When you are kind to a woman in a strip club, it surprises her, catches her off guard. When she finds out you're a Jesus follower she's even more taken aback; when you tell her you're there to spread a little love, wish her a good night, and offer her support she cannot believe her ears.

It's this kind of culture shocking, world tipping, radical love ministry Jesus taught us as he walked and talked and healed and cast out demons across the Galilee and in the Jerusalem precinct. In John's Gospel we have a beautiful story of Jesus being confronted with a woman caught in adultery, brought to him by her accusers who demand Jesus' response (John 8:1–11). Jesus has just come from the temple and astonishes the guilty woman and the mob when he bends down and begins to write in the dirt. Though we can't be sure, I wonder if the woman suspected Jesus to be stooping down to gather dust to mix with liquid in order to prepare the noxious tonic prescribed by the Law intended to determine guilt or innocence for women caught in adultery (Num 5:11–31). But he doesn't. There is no truth serum, no forced confession, only a question to those who have brought her to him, a probing as to their own sin. When the angry mob clears since they too have sinned, she is left alone with Jesus who tells her he does not accuse her, and she should "go and sin no more" (John 8:11).

In this pericope Jesus is teaching us a grand example of ministry for our times. He intentionally left the temple courts and made his way out to the people and instead of doling out judgment he adjusted his posture and got into the dirt where the woman lay. He risked himself to be for and with her in her vulnerability. He took the ancient practice of judgement and turned it into hope.

The paradigm of ministry where we worship in our auditorium-like churches located in the affluent part of town and invite the broken, the weak, the downtrodden, the economically oppressed, the stripper, the bar maid, the homeless man to come to our church because of our great music and relevant programming is over—if it ever existed. We live in such a time that those who have been abused and cast out by this life are convinced the church is anything but loving and does anything but care. Ministries of reconciliation must be built on the paradigm of Christ. They must risk, they must get low and enter into the dark alleys and back-door clubs and begin to write love in the dust.

Sex Trafficking and Strip Clubs

When we began visiting a local strip club near our church we knew nothing about sex trafficking. At the time, I had heard the term but only understood it to be an issue overseas. Sex trafficking, I thought, happened in India and the Philippines. I had no idea it was happening in the small town where I lived. The US Government defines sex trafficking as "A commercial sex act induced by force, fraud, or coercion, or in which the person induced to perform such act has not attained 18 years of age."[1] It has been my experience that most women who work in the sex trade are in the trade for reasons of force, fraud or coercion, though few will admit it outside the bonds of hard-won friendship. In fact, we now know that 70 percent of women who are trafficked are working in the sex trade.[2] This means that the singular most consolidated venue for trafficking in domestic cases is the strip club, which may as well be called the sex club, as these clubs function as fronts for the real trade that goes on inside. This means sex trafficking is happening in your city and mine.

1. National Institute of Justice, "Human Trafficking."
2. Trafficking.org, "Statistics."

Though 89 percent of women working in the sex trade would get out if they believed it was possible, that is often not what they portray publicly.[3] Unfortunately, what routinely turns out to be the case is that women are incredibly bound to their oppressors such that in Stripped Love's work we have found the term *pimp* is almost always synonymous with *boyfriend*. Though women in the sex industry might come to the work though a myriad of circumstances and scenarios, what often proves the common factor is the presence of a partner who is benefiting from her work in the club.

Strikingly, we find that in many cases family and friends function as *recruiters* and work to groom women, girls, and some young men into *the life*. Even as I write this essay, an arrest was just made in my city in a local motel where young women had been dropped off by their parents to meet men and engage in sex for sale. In this instance and in many others like them, the parents are the pimps. This is an example of how we sometimes see generational poverty lived out in broken communities.

In a whole host of other scenarios, women come to the life because of addiction. A fierce need for drugs and alcohol keeps them dependent upon providers and pushers such that selling their bodies becomes the logical solution for a steady supply. Unfortunately, women in this arena become used up and abandoned early in life. My team and I just attended the funeral of a forty-seven-year-old mother and grandmother whose outward appearance reflected the harsh realities of life in the trade.

Still other women come to the sex trade by means of the Internet. Pornographic and escort services are seducing and hiring women to sell themselves online. One ad I recently viewed, targeted to exotic dancers, said, "No transportation no problem, put your skills to work online." Countless numbers of other victims have reported being lured by someone online whom they thought they would begin dating. The relationship became sexual and then possessive and then abusive and then she found herself doing things for money she never thought she could do. Perhaps even more troubling, we are now learning pimps are recruiting in shelters where women are recovering from having hit rock bottom. Facilities filled with women who have lost all hope have proven to be fertile ground to promote and recruit women into the trade. Traffickers, pimps, and commercial sex clubs prey on women in desperate situations and seek them out in the most vulnerable circumstances. This is why small, economically deprived towns still have booming sex clubs within the city limits and why you will

3. Farley, "Prostitution and Trafficking in Nine Countries."

find clubs and escort services and Internet sex sites serving communities with colleges and universities.

When Poverty is Your Pimp

Part of the struggle in operating a nonprofit ministry for women who are trafficked and exploited by the commercial sex industry is that most people are unaware of the plight of the women and families and communities who are affected. In short, it can be difficult to convince outsiders looking in, persons who live in the upscale neighborhoods and attend the megachurch to have concern for women whom they believe seduce men for money every night. An uneducated public can sometimes heartlessly assume that persons who work in the sex industry are there predominantly because they have chosen to do so and because they are making a healthy daily income in this lascivious employ. Incumbent then on our ministry and others like us is to inform the church and society about the realities of life in the sex trade.

In most instances, women who work as exotic dancers are contract workers who walk away with only their tips at the end of the night. Dancers take rotations on stage and perform for tips and entertain in so-called VIP back rooms for additional compensation. Out of their tips, dancers are also expected to pay the *house.* This means, no matter what a dancer might earn on a given night, an exorbitant amount is being paid out to the bartender, wait staff, disc jockey, doorman, security, etc. In the small, low-rent clubs in my town, for instance, where a dancer might make as little as $20 per night, she is still responsible for paying the house at least $50 per night. As earning a living wage happens to be a critical need for most women in the trade, women can regularly be found leaving with customers, and continuing on after a shift to private parties arranged by staff to earn extra money. Thus, strip clubs are a gateway to prostitution.

Add to the above the systemic realities of generational poverty. Most of the women I work with live well below the poverty line and have for most of their lives. In many cases, they were trafficked as children, abused in the foster care system, or their mothers were sex workers themselves. These women don't have driver's licenses and have limited access to transportation, plus they are paid in cash so they don't file taxes. Most of them don't have health insurance, not because it's not offered to them but because they don't have the necessary paperwork to file. As many of these women are perennially homeless, couch surfing from one friend's place to the next, without adequate resources for childcare, their children, already at risk, are often left with less than suitable supervision.

Persons who work in this arena long enough become painfully aware of the cyclical nature of poverty, abuse, trafficking, and sex work. Intervention is badly needed at all points in the scenario. In the commercial sex trade women are overwhelmingly *trauma bound* to their oppressors and are victims of abuse from a young age while parenting children themselves and recruiting others for the life.

Beyond Rescue to Joined Lives

As with any other nonprofit cause, people are always interested in results and want to know how many women we've helped transition out. The truth is, over the course of more than six years now, we've helped several women find life outside of the trade—and for that we give thanks as we recognize this as the work of the Spirit in and through us for the good of our sisters. However, we are clear that our mission lies in the connection. Our success is measured in friendship. Every single time a woman invites us to sit with her in her pain, become family with her, knitting our broken hearts with hers, we believe it is a win and from here we leave it to Jesus.

Though we have aided women who needed emergency extraction from life-threatening situations, we've also lost women to drugs and alcohol and to the power of fear that keeps them bound. We are clear then that we are not rescuers; rather, we are broken women who are called to love other broken women, just like God loves us all—right where we are, just as we are. When the mission is to just show up consistently, bringing all of who you are and love, friendships are born and over time are nurtured into transformational bonds that can be stronger than those holding a woman to unhealthy relationships and practices.

It becomes clear soon after entering a strip club that your reason for patronage must be made evident. Because women in the industry are certainly at risk, in competition with one another, compartmentalized, and often under the influence of a substance, assessments are quickly made of strangers in their midst. This is precisely why random and sporadic visits to a variety of clubs proves fruitless. Women in the sex industry are skeptical and reluctant with regard to other women who are not paying customers and are otherwise unknown to them. It is paramount then in ministry to women in the sex trade that persons committed to this work first prove themselves to be safe people through consistent presence and support. Trust can only be established and nurtured through authentic community.

The importance of vested ministry rooted in authentic community cannot be overstated. This is why short-term work projects or drop-in service days are typically unable to create lasting impact in this context. While there are all sorts of well-meaning organizations that try this approach, because of the realities of life for women in the sex trade, it is rarely effective and more damaging than helpful. It must also be said that attempting to build faux relationships as some sort of technique will fail every time. These women have become experts at scoping out and reading the people who come into their midst, because their lives depend upon it. In most cases, their lives are a string of shattered relationships, so they are reluctant to open themselves again. Just as in my initial encounter with Heaven, until you get down into the grit of shared lives there is really no engagement. As with any friendship, you find places of equal footing, you serve one another, you call out the dignity in each other, and both lives are enriched because both parties are invested in knowing and being known. I cannot ask my friends to open their lives to me if I am unwilling to share mine with them. I cannot ask them to share their needs if I'm not ready to share likewise. My friends have stood with me through grief and loss, offered prayers on my behalf when my mother was sick in the hospital. I have shared the deep struggle of infertility with these friends and they celebrated the birth and adoption of my son with jubilation. We have thrown countless baby showers and swapped clothes back and forth. We have visited in the hospital and funeral homes, we have attended each other's birthday parties and holiday celebrations. Just as I am given a seat of honor in the clubs where I visit in my town, I extend the same esteem when my friends traverse to places on my so-called turf. In our exercise class held in my home church, our friends from the club are admitted without charge, just as we are now admitted into their clubs. Across the years and the stories, amidst the trials and betrayals, in the busted up broken places and in the happy, lovely moments we have become family. Thus, we do all the things a family does; we eat and drink, we cry and laugh, we support and hold accountable, we sit in the mess and scream at the top of our lungs at the commencement service. We show up. We just love.

While it would be inauthentic to paint a portrait of perfection here, we are eternally grateful for the opportunity to live out the call of reconciliation in our community. Like all other gospel work, we take two steps forward and nineteen backwards. But this is good work, and the purpose of our call in Christ Jesus.

Bibliography

Farley, Melissa. "Prostitution and Trafficking in Nine Countries: An Update on Violence and Posttraumatic Stress Disorder." http://www.prostitutionresearch.com.

National Institute of Justice. "Human Trafficking." http://www.nij.gov/topics/crime/human-trafficking/pages/welcome.aspx.

Trafficking.org. "Statistics." http://www.trafficking.org/learn/statistics.aspx.

— Chapter 10 —

Self-Care
A Whole New Way of Being

Katheryn L. W. Heinz

It was already an hour past my kids' bedtime and their energy levels far exceeded mine. Frustrated by the long day, frustrated by the long work night ahead, and frustrated that I had asked them too many times to pick up their room, I bent down to pick up a stray bookmark. I stood up with all of the power of that frustration and was met with a piercing blow to the back of my head. In my frantic attempt to pull everything together, I had slammed my head into the corner of a piece of furniture.

I dropped to the floor, crawled to the couch in the back room, and focused on breathing through the throbbing, nausea, and dizziness. The next morning, I had an important meeting with a team of consultants to set the direction for the ministry I co-founded. I tried to pull cohesive thoughts through the mental fog and splitting headache. I tried to form sentences that made sense. I tried to act like nothing was wrong. I tried to ignore the fact that I clearly had a concussion. It was a pivotal time in my ministry and I definitely did not have time for this.

I didn't make it through that strategic meeting. My screaming head and nausea wouldn't allow me. Everyone agreed that I needed immediate medical care. A visit to the doctor confirmed our suspicions. Then came the second blow. Under doctor's orders I had to go on complete brain rest. I sat on the examination table listening to what she meant by "brain rest" and my bewilderment turned into anxiety that turned into fear. My professional "has-it-all-together" facade began to crack. I cried.

I couldn't work, couldn't watch the kids, couldn't read, couldn't watch TV. I wasn't even supposed to *think* while I was lying down. I told the doctor that I needed to make a plan with my co-director to cover my absence, and she said that was against the rules, too. I imagined a million details unraveling. If I were honest though, I was also terrified that I didn't know how to be completely still. For three days, I laid on that couch in the back room. For three days I had to deal with that which I usually ignore . . . myself. It was the beginning of a whole new way of being.

The past fifteen years of my life have been dedicated to the intentional, Christian practices of justice and reconciliation. I've worked in the church, the academy, and the community. I've served as researcher, advocate, cultural mediator, adjunct professor, and activist. My husband tells me that I don't know how to rest. Once, one of my students came up to me in concern, and told me that she noticed that I don't breathe. My best form of rest is switching gears to work on something else. I have been consumed with drive, vision, responsibility, stress, and feelings of inadequacy. I have ended up physically sick, mentally spent, not having any tangible sense of God in my life, and wondering if all this sacrifice for ministry was worth it.

Self-care is not something that is natural to me, and I am definitely not an expert on the topic. However, I've spent quite a bit of time working out self-care in my life, and in my obvious weakness, God is clearly teaching me some things.

I used to think that self-care was a protected time away from stress and responsibilities, and it sounded great. I had plans for reading books, or to meet up with a friend, or for a quiet retreat. People would encourage me to get a hobby or to discover how I best liked to treat myself. That type of self-care only existed in my imagination, rarely on my calendar. When I did indulge in time away, the first part of my time was spent in detox from the stress and the last part was spent in preparing myself to re-enter the fray. What remained in the middle was a paltry amount of refreshment that quickly disappeared. There were times that I came back with more resentment of what was in front of me than renewal.

I have come to realize, though, that I don't find self-care in rest. I find rest in self-care. Avoidance of self-care isn't being too busy or unbalanced.

The avoidance of self-care is actually the fragmentation of self, a disintegration of relationship with God, and a distortion of purpose. Self-care is not a retreat from ministry, rather it is the womb from which ministry is born.

If we believe that the ministry of reconciliation is rooted in the oneness we find in Christ (Col 3:11), and that the practice of reconciliation involves tearing down walls of hostility (Eph 2:14–16), we must begin that ministry of reconciliation within ourselves. Self-care becomes less about pampering and more about reconciling. Self-care becomes less about rest from ministry and more about finding God and our true selves in the midst of ministry. Without reconciliation within ourselves, we cannot hope to work towards reconciliation among each other. In order to move forward in any kind of meaningful ministry, I had to first figure out this thing called self-care. I now understand self-care to be itself a ministry of reconciliation, the reconciling of identity, significance, and vocation.

Identity

If we are talking about self-care, it's important to know exactly what "self" is. At your core, your very essence, the center of your being, who are you?

On one hand, we embody various roles in our life. For example, I am a sister, a wife, a mom, a daughter, a friend, an administrator, a teacher, a neighbor. We also embody certain characteristics. I am creative, driven, energetic, and not one bit athletic. I'm female, curly haired, arguably middle-aged, and white. We can also be described by the talents or activities we enjoy. I love art, estate sales, and great food. I used to sing jazz and play tenor saxophone, and I'm becoming reacquainted with *Candy Land* and *Mary Poppins* through my kids.

If you step back and think about your descriptors, you can see ones that you exhibit every day, the ones that shaped your past, the ones you defend dearly, and the ones you hold lightly. These descriptors are God's gifts to us, the things he has given in unique combination to each of us. Though in reality, those things that make us uniquely us aren't actually us. We exist outside these things.

I was asked once how someone could possibly separate oneself from one's gifts. How is it possible to exist outside of what makes us uniquely us? The answer rests in the experience of a parent who loses an only child, the experience of a musician who loses the use of his hands, the experience of a poet who loses her ability to form words. Life goes on, even when the special things that make us feel most like *us* are ripped away. Can we possibly exist without the things that we think we are? The answer has to be yes.

When we don't recognize that we are separate from our descriptors, we confuse our gifts with our very being. To believe that those descriptors shape our essential core is a terrible lie that keeps us from knowing our true selves. When life changes and we don't get to enjoy our gifts, we feel as if pieces of ourselves are missing. When life gets unsustainably busy, we assume that our gifts will get us through, and we wonder why we feel less than whole. When someone criticizes us or competes with us, we take it too personally. When we feel inadequate to the task, we feel undesirable and maybe even detestable.

Equating self with gifts amounts to segmenting ourselves into little fragments of being that light up when utilized and grow dim when not. We become a collection of descriptors that are precariously joined together, but we are not whole. Our perception of self becomes only as deep and wide as the descriptors we carry.

Significance

Five years ago, my husband and I found ourselves four hours into a nine-hour drive in the middle of a winter storm. The ice on the road made it difficult to complete our journey to Grand Rapids, but the obstacles we were experiencing in ministry at that time felt all the more daunting. In both travel and ministry, we had gone too far to turn around, but we were not terribly confident about facing what was ahead. We were relieved when we finally arrived safely, and we had a wonderful weekend with our good friends who had planted an urban, multicultural church there.

The sermon that my friend preached that weekend was a gift that has spoken into my life years beyond that snowy weekend in Michigan. It was centered on Jesus' teaching on abiding in the vine in John 15. She proclaimed that we will produce abundant fruit if we focus on abiding in the vine, because the vine is the source of the fruit. But this proclamation came with the warning that if we focus on the fruit we can become disconnected from the vine completely and not even notice until the fruit withers away. We, as the branch, will wither with it.[1]

I suddenly realized that I had not only put too much focus on the fruit, I had actually built a fruit stand. As a couple who raised all of our

1. Lipscomb, Sermon, January 16, 2011.

own salary and ministry costs, we were often put in situations where people wanted to see our fruit, and examine it for variety, quality, and quantity. It is a horrible way to live and a horrible way to serve, yet the fruit stand model of support raising and accountability is a common and devastating cause of people in ministry leaving the vine for the sake of the fruit.

Whereas I have confused my true identity with what I thought was my identity, I have also confused my significance with what I produced and contributed. If the significance and worth of my ministry efforts were assessed (rightly or wrongly) by my fruit, then I also saw my own significance and worth in my fruit.

Fruit, however, never springs forth from sheer willpower of the branch. It can only spring forth from the vine through the branch. When we put the center of our energy and concern on the quantity and quality of our contributions, we cut ourselves off from our root, the vine, our God. We are no longer living as children of God, but as little ministry factories. We become dis-integrated from our true source of significance and we naturally fall apart.

Vocation

Merriam-Webster defines vocation as "a summons or strong inclination to a particular state or course of action; especially: a divine call to the religious life," "the work in which a person is employed," and "the special function of an individual or group."[2] While our vocations can include our job responsibilities, the whole concept of vocation extends beyond our tasks and begins to define our purpose.

As Christians we have big visions of how things are supposed to be. Revelation 21:4 describes a new heaven and new earth without tears, death, mourning, crying, or pain. That is not the world I see around me, though I know that it is the reality of the kingdom come. We as disciples go out to bear witness of this reality, becoming as a servant, restoring relationships, healing pain, fighting injustice, building systems of equity, and offering hope in impossible situations. The fulfillment of all these things are far beyond the capabilities of any human or any combination of humans. Yet, our vocation, our calling, is to participate in these things with the expectation that they are not only ideals, but trusted promises.

2. Merriam-Webster.com. "Vocation."

Whenever you place yourself in the crossroads of relational tension and resolve to pull the chasm together, pulling the edges of relationship over the rocky ground of historic systems of mistrust, divisiveness, and pain, you will get scraped up in the process. While we might be vessels of God's redeeming work in the world, we are not so strong as to personally hold every pain and tension we encounter. Nor can we possibly know how to adequately understand or attend to all of those pains and tensions.

We are David up against Goliath. We are Lazarus already four days gone in a tomb. We are disciples sent out with the buddy system to cast out demons when we can't even catch fish. It doesn't matter how much education, experience, wisdom, creativity, connections, resources, passion, or compassion we have, we simply cannot "bring the kingdom of God." It is not ours to bring.

For those of us who have been socially and politically active in our faith this is a confusing vocation. Christians are not called to complacency nor complicity with the broken status quo. Yet if it is not our vocation to fully make it right then what are we doing? What is our function? What's the point? Are we to keep running towards this beautiful new heaven and new earth, only to continually experience it as a mirage that vanishes in our immediacy but appears once again as a promise just out of reach in the distance? That kind of thinking is at the least discouraging. It can become vocationally paralyzing and spiritually suicidal.

When we start confusing God's work with our own we lose perspective. The lens through which we understand our vocation becomes a carnival mirror, bent and shaped around our immediate experiences and responsibilities, distorting what we understand our vocation and purpose to be. This distortion steals our freedom to live, serve, work, and rest in the middle of God's creation.

Finding Our Way

David Bosch, one of the most influential missiologists of the twentieth century, wrote that there are two dangers facing those in ministry. "We can either content ourselves with the rut we're in and have complete peace of mind about it or we can urge ourselves on madly and relentlessly. There is a third way, however: that of living in a gentle tension between giving ourselves in full surrender to our fellow man, yet at the same time enjoying the peace of the Lord."[3] This is what self-care in ministry looks like. We must find our way back to the peace of the Lord in the middle of pressing forward—and experience joy in the process.

When self-care isn't observed we begin to spiral. Eventually, everything feels out of control. The steps to find your way back to peace and joy are simple: Get centered. Get God. Get honest.

Get Centered

If you have ever thrown clay on a potter's wheel you know the importance of centering. Centering is the process of getting your clay perfectly positioned on the wheel so that it doesn't wobble in any direction. Professional potters make this look easy, but someone new to the wheel will tell you that it is difficult and frustrating. The temptation is to get it *mostly* centered. Once the clay looks centered and isn't wobbling as much, the new potter often starts bringing up the sides to shape the piece of pottery. Without perfectly centered clay, you are constantly fighting against the wayward movements of the clay. The best you can hope to get is an uneven vessel, but most often you get an imploded mess on the wheel. Once the clay is centered you don't fight the piece as much. Getting the clay centered is the most crucial part of getting a beautifully shaped piece with even sides and good structural integrity. Centered clay makes throwing pottery a lot more fun.

My journey to rediscovering myself started with letting go of myself, five minutes at a time, in daily contemplative prayer. Contemplative prayer is nothing new and is in fact one of those practices that unites communities of faith through space and time from around the world and throughout history. The ins and outs of contemplative prayer are readily found in books, retreats, and internet resources, and can be explained by those who are much more experienced than I. However, I can tell you that it has become an anchor for me.

There seems to be a movement among Christian activists. We've realized that we can't do this alone or maybe at all. But miracles still bloom around us, and staying centered on the Creator of miracles allows us to breathe new life into ourselves and into our service to him and others around us. I have learned that contemplative prayer, while looking like sitting around and doing nothing, is actually a discipline of recentering, a practice just as essential as centering clay.

3. Bosch, *A Spirituality of the Road*, 23.

Before we can have an image of our true self, we must experience ourselves as nothing. We are but a lump of clay in the hands of our Creator God to be formed into his will. Thomas Merton wrote that:

> . . . all our meditation should begin with the realization of our nothingness and helplessness in the presence of God. . . . But one reason why our meditation never gets started is perhaps that we never make this real, serious return to the center of our own nothingness before God. Hence we never enter into the deepest reality of our relationship with him. In other words we meditate merely 'in the mind,' in the imagination, or at best in the desires, considering religious truths from a detached objective viewpoint. We do not begin by seeking to "find our heart," that is to sink into a deep awareness of the ground of our identity before God and in God. "Finding our heart" and recovering this awareness of our inmost identity implies the recognition that our external, everyday self is to a great extent a mask and a fabrication. It is not our true self. And indeed our true self is not easy to find. It is hidden in obscurity and "nothingness," at the center where we are in direct dependence on God. But since the reality of all Christian meditation depends on this recognition, our attempt to meditate without it is in fact self-contradictory. It is like trying to walk without feet.[4]

In taking time to find our center in Christ through the emptying of ourselves and refocusing on him, we start to restore our understanding of who we are at our core and reset ourselves towards God. A nourished self is not the full enjoyment of one's every gift, but the ability to set them down and say, I am enough without them. God is enough. I am enough.

When we find our center and start valuing our real selves, we can begin to value our gifts as they are. Knowing that our descriptors are both distinct from us and unique to us allows us to both enjoy them and refrain from them. We are free to draw close and set aside. It is this realization that allows us to set things aside each week and rest for a full day, knowing that whatever comes from our unplugged selves, it is okay. We are able to have a richer life because of them and not feel beholden to them. We can be shaped by them, but not defined by them. Our centered clay can then be made beautiful through our gifts by our Creator, and our unique vessel can take various shapes of beauty over time.

4. Merton, *Contemplative Prayer*, 48–49.

Get God

The process of centering gives us a peaceful place, and we find ourselves emotionally dwelling in the center of God's good design for us instead of the chaos around us. We start feeling freedom in losing the baggage that can weigh us down. It feels good to feel centered. However, it becomes way too easy to get comfortable, and then we immediately get back in trouble. It is not enough to get centered. You have got to get God.

In the beginning, Adam and Eve were dwelling in the center of God's good design. Adam and Eve had much freedom in the garden and everything was pretty fantastic. The only limit they had was the tree of the knowledge of good and evil. The linchpin to keeping this good design was trusting God, and in doing so, accepting this limit. The failure to accept their limit came through the tempting idea that maybe they didn't really need a limit. Maybe they wouldn't actually die. Maybe it would be nice to be a little more like God. Maybe God didn't grasp all that they could really handle.

As the people of God working towards reconciliation and justice, we have much creative freedom to join Jesus in his redemptive work, but we have our limits. We must rest and have a real Sabbath. We are to love our enemies, even those promoting injustice. We have to realize that there are many things we aren't capable of fixing and many things we don't have control over. None of these limits sound reasonable or good when we are trying to battle systems of injustice or trying to mediate and reconcile divided people. The temptation is to think that certainly those limits don't apply to all of this important work that can't wait. Let's not make the same Eden mistake. Instead, get God.

When I say "get God," I mean that we have to trust God, we have to recognize that only God is God, and we have to experience God being God. Recognizing our limits allows us to do these things. Ignoring our limits means that we aren't trusting God's good design. We aren't trusting God to show up. We aren't trusting God to know what is best for us. We aren't trusting God with our reputation, our status, our provision, our responsibilities. We aren't trusting God to handle God's own kingdom. We have some kind of crazy idea that blasting through our limits will somehow get us to where we want to be.

Having limits doesn't mean that we are weak or insufficient. Having limits means that we are human. When Adam and Eve chose to go beyond their limits, they didn't fall down dead in the moment, but they lost their freedom to enjoy being fully human in the midst of God's creation. Instead of living freely in their vocation as caretakers of creation, they became vulnerable, afraid, and experienced the pain of their labor. We also experience the pain of our labor if we do not recognize our limits. Instead of our gifts serving us as we serve God, we expect God to step in and restore us so that we can serve our gifts. We become fixated on that which our hands have made, or could make, instead of seeing God create amazing, wondrous, and miraculous things.

Our embrace of limitations allows us accept our vocation to participate in God's reconciling work, but not bear the full responsibility to fulfill it. Limitations allow us to stop, rest, and trust. We become restored in ground allowed to go fallow, if even for a lunch break, an evening with friends, or a weekly Sabbath.

Recognizing that God already knows our limitations allows us to go boldly into callings that we know are completely beyond us. As we stop at the end of ourselves and before all that we wish we could be, we are forced to confront the mystery of God. We experience his grace, power, and creation. We can once again enjoy our work as vocation, because our previously distorted vocation is now reconciled within the context of God's larger work. The kingdom of God is being birthed with us or without us. Yet, we are among the many midwives called to participate in this birth.

Get Honest

When our identities, significance, and vocation are fragmented and distorted, we live in fear. If we begin to reconcile those by getting centered and getting God, we are freed from the fear of being honest. So much emotional, physical, and spiritual energy is wasted in avoiding the reality of difficulties. There is great healing in honesty.

Stress is the distance stretched between expectations (placed upon us by ourselves, our governing structures, and/or the people around us) and the reality of our circumstances. We feel good when expectations are met, but when expectations and reality are far apart, the internal splintering we feel is stress. Burnout is the natural extension of stress that goes unchecked. Burnout isn't doing too much without rest. Burnout is attempting to do too much without support, resources, or ability. Burnout happens when there is extreme and prolonged stress in an environment where expectations are impossible to meet. Much of the clinical research on occupational burnout points to its cause in the disillusionment found among highly motivated people. Basically, deeply compassionate people with high ideals working in a broken world get disillusioned, feel like a failure, and then burn out. The aftermath is emotional exhaustion, relational numbness, and a feeling of professional inadequacy.

Christians who work in ministry related to reconciliation and justice go out into the world carrying not only the highest ideals of what could be—we go into the world fully expecting it to become reality. It is the largest of expectations. After awhile, we realize that we know even less than we thought we did when we started, and self-doubt creeps in. As you grow in understanding of other people, and your understanding of the world grows more complicated and expansive, fewer people understand you. Your support wanes along with your own self-confidence. When success is perceived to be nothing short of the kingdom come, and we feel responsible and insignificant, stress is inevitable and burnout is common.

Without honesty, the enormous distance between expectations and reality becomes the elephant in the room. We don't know what to do with the distance, so we ignore it. But what if we aren't called to cure that great divide? Henri Nouwen writes that there is a difference between care and cure. "Cure means 'change.' . . . But cure, desirable as it may be, can easily become violent, manipulative, and even destructive if it does not grow out of care. Care is being with, crying out with, suffering with, feeling with. Care is compassion."[5] Our personal quest to cure the world can turn into a neglect of care of ourselves and others. Honesty allows us to shift back to our true vocation of being caretakers of creation not "cure-takers."

I cannot tell you how many ministry practitioners find themselves in impromptu support groups. Someone lets their guard slip, their vulnerability exposed, and the room is discovered to be safe. The rest of the conversation is a dog pile of shared experiences, hurts, feelings of failure, doubt, fear. Honesty allows us to reframe our stress into an opportunity to grow.

Honesty is not the same thing as complaining. Honesty takes a good look at the mountain of expectations and names them out loud. Honesty takes a good look at where we are in relation to that mountain and claims it. Honesty gives language to the obstacles in our way. Honesty then says, "If I can't reach the top of impossible, how can I creatively get around this obstacle in front of me?" Honesty gives us the opportunity to respect and

---

5. Nouwen, *Bread for the Journey,* 40.

work towards our ideals, but set better personal expectations so that we can move forward.

By instilling care in our current situations instead of hammering the expectations of cure, we start to reconcile the tensions, repair the splinters, and bring closer together those things that are far apart. Be honest with what is going on, and let it sit there for a bit. See that the world didn't end. We can trust that God has a good handle on the end goal. We just need care in our incremental moves forward, reconciling tensions within us as we work towards reconciling the tensions around us.

Being honest brings fresh air for new solutions and possibilities. It also brings an acceptance of the "less than successful," which is the only place where learning happens. When our desire for discovery is greater than our fear of failure, we are no longer held captive, and we create an environment for self-care. In fact, it is not possible for anyone to fully experience self-care in an environment that does not promote the care of self. We must protect one another more than our illusions of perfection.

Perhaps in no other way is the community aspect of self-care more evident than in the caring of our realities in the midst of stress. Community that encourages honesty and feels comfortable in care without cure allows us all to be more valuable than the outcomes that we all long for. Whether the community is family, church, friends, or work, we discover that self-care is never to be experienced in isolation. Self-care is a team sport.

A Whole New Way of Being

Self-care requires rhythms of practice that reinforce our reconciliation of identity, significance, and vocation. We need daily and weekly times of rest. We need periodic and seasonal times of retreat and renewal. Every seven years or so, we need to take extended leaves or sabbaticals to the best our situations will allow. These rhythms are not additions to our schedule, rather they provide scaffolding within our schedule, making sure that we are getting centered, getting God, and getting honest. These rhythms rewire our gut reactions to our immediate life encounters. Our internal compass starts automatically pointing to self-care in the middle of chaos. We no longer react out of our old means of coping. We have a whole new way of being. The fruit of reconciliation that we feel growing within us gives us new resolve to participate in God's ministry of reconciliation around us.

Bibliography

Bosch, David J. *A Spirituality of the Road*. Eugene, OR: Wipf & Stock, 1979.

Lipscomb, Christy. Sermon: City Life Church. Grand Rapids, January 16, 2011.

Maslach, Christina, and Susan E. Jackson. "Burnout in Organizational Settings." *Applied Social Psychology Annual*, Vol. 5 (1984) 133–53.

Merton, Thomas. *Contemplative Prayer*. New York: Image, 1969.

Nouwen, Henri. *Bread for the Journey*. New York: HarperCollins, 1997.

Pines, Ayala M. "Burnout: An Existential Perspective." In *Professional Burnout: Recent Developments in Theory and Research,* edited by Wilma B. Schaufeli, Christina Maslach, and Tadeusz Marek, 33–52. Philadelphia: Taylor & Francis, 1993.